FAVORITE RECIPES® PRESENTS:

Medley of MEATS

A Cookbook With
A Musical Flair

© Favorite Recipes Press/NASHVILLE EMS MCMLXXVII
Post Office Box 77, Nashville, Tennessee 37202
Library of Congress Cataloging in Publication Data
Main entry under title:
Favorite Recipes Press Presents Medley of Meats,
A Cookbook With A Musical Flair
    Includes index.
    1. Cookery (Meat) I. Favorite Recipes Press.
II. Title: Medley of meats.
TX749.F378   641.6'6   77-11204
ISBN 0-87197-116-X
0 9 8 7 6 5 4 3 2 1

DEAR PATRON

What better selection to follow the all-round favorite KITCHEN AUDITIONS, than a musical MEDLEY OF MEATS. Everyone loves meats of all kinds. This Cookbook is designed to keep you in tempo with the biggest hits in meats recipes.

Young music lovers, through the sale of this captivating Cookbook, are encouraging their many Patrons to continue contributions to their local school music groups. Their enthusiasm and your generous support are two elements necessary for continued interest in the wholesome activities of our young people today.

This Cookbook will be a colorful addition to your own cookbook library. Also, the next time someone asks, "May I have your recipe?" offer her the opportunity of buying this edition for her own collection. Remember, everyone benefits from these sales!

Sincerely,

Mary Jane Blount
Editor

Nicky Beaulieu
Project Manager

Board of Advisors

Earl Dunn
Muncie, Indiana
School of Music, Ball State University
Past President, National Band Association

George S. Howard, USAF Col. (RET)
San Antonio, Texas
Former Director, United States Air Force Band
Past President, American Band Masters
 Association

William Ledue
Coral Gables, Florida
President, Florida Music Educators Association

Bill Sloan
Huntsville, Alabama
President, Alabama Band Association

Dr. W. J. Julian
Director of Bands
University of Tennessee

Contents

Meats In Harmony
A Cookbook With A Musical Flair

Homemakers everywhere know that meats are most often the high note in their favorite family and party menus. Whether a meal features fried chicken or roast beef, fresh-cooked shrimp or grilled trout, barbecued pork or smoked wild game, aromatic and flavorful meats are sure to strike a harmonious chord with any family's favorite vegetable or side dish accompaniment. No other food can turn a casserole into a concert, be the star in a salad, soup or sandwich, or create the full fanfare of flavors from the oven or grill in the way nature's medley of meats is able to do.

Americans are virtuosos in the preparation and enjoyment of meats, and for very good cause. The forests, fields, and waters of North America have historically produced a perfect harmony of seafood and freshwater fish, as well as plenty of wild fowl and hearty game animals. Moreover, modern American farms provide an abundance of the world's most succulent beef, poultry, and pork. Homemakers in the early days of American history were faced with meats that, by today's standards, were not only scarce, but unpalatable, as well. Still, she knew just how to marinate a tough cut of beef, stew a stringy barnyard chicken, or braise a half-wild pig until it was savory, tender, and satisfying. It would be very unusual for a modern homemaker to worry about the quality of the meat she buys because today's meat and poultry industries market the very best product. Moreover, today's recipes are far easier to prepare and are far more diversified than ever before. They also reflect a superb blend of tested methods, unique flavor additions, and the special touches of an international concert of cooks who have come to America from countries the world over in the past 200 years.

Even the best of food experts would find it hard to say which meat is the most popular on American tables. Beef, which is typically more expensive than poultry and pork, still out-sells the other meats. It is important to note, however, that beef sales include the purchases of ground beef, whose all-around usefulness is unmatched. As a rule, chicken and turkey are the most economical poultry, as well as the most economical meats, and their sales run a very close second to the sale of beef cuts. Historically, pork has been the most commonly consumed meat, because it was so easy to preserve during long travels and cold winters. It seems that there is really no accurate way to measure the quantities of wild game, fowl, and fish that are consumed each year, but judging from the popularity of hunting and fishing, the amount is probably surprisingly large. There is no doubt that homemakers will always include a lively selection of meat, poultry, and fish or shellfish in the meals they plan, and for a very simple and undeniable reason — their families want it that way!

Assured of the quality of meat and of her recipes, the most important concern of today's homemaker is getting the most in flavor and nutrition for the best price. Meat provides only 10% of the nutrition we need, yet it takes up as much as 25 to 30% of the dollar we spend on food, making wise meat budgeting a must. When buying meat, know what you are paying per serving, not just per pound. For example, a boneless canned ham may seem extravagantly priced. But, this "expensive" canned ham is really the better buy because it serves 5 persons per pound, while a picnic ham serves only 2 persons per pound. Ground beef is another good example. Cheaper ground beef contains far more fat than the more costly "extra lean" ground beef, ground chuck, or ground round, and as a result, loses volume during cooking due to the loss of fat. So, when used for hamburgers or meat loaves, the more expensive ground meat is the better buy. Cheaper ground beef is usually the more economical for meat sauces, casseroles, or soups and stews. The best buys in pork, veal, lamb, and fresh fish are often found in specialty or ethnic grocery stores, rather than in supermarkets. Germans favor top-quality pork, Italians prefer veal, and Greeks love lamb, so the stores that cater to these groups will often have the best quality meat and fish selections at the lowest prices.

Poultry has a distinct, mild flavor that goes well with almost any sauce, salad, or side dish. It is available the year-round, and is always economical and packed with nutrition. Poultry is also very calorie-wise, if you are watching your weight. It should be pointed out that even though a whole chicken is usually cheaper per pound, it is not always the best buy. If your family will not eat certain parts of the whole chicken (such as the wings, the back, or the gizzards), then you should buy the packages that contain only the parts of the chicken they *will* eat. The more expensive packages will be cheaper in the long run, giving the most satisfaction without needless waste. Turkey is another unbeatable poultry product, as there is hardly another meat that offers a combination of flavor, elegance and economy in one penny-wise package. Of course, a golden, roast turkey is the traditional entree for most American Thanksgiving and Christmas dinners, but it shouldn't be limited to that by any means. Turkey is both plentiful and cheap in the late fall and cooked or uncooked, it freezes quite well. Thawed and served as turkey salad, turkey casserole, or even turkey slices with gravy, this regal American bird can add some welcomed diversity to many summer, spring and winter meals.

The family lucky enough to have a successful hunter in its midst can enjoy an abundant variety of wild game and fowl on its menus. Quail, dove, duck, and pheasant are gourmet treats that appeal to the taste of every family member. Each has its own hearty, wild flavor that makes every single one a special and unique experience. Game meats are another very traditional part of American eating, yet many modern cooks avoid preparing it for fear it will turn out too strong in flavor, or dry and tough. Because wild game animals are naturally leaner and stronger than domesticated animals, their meat is sinewy and less tender — *before cooking*. But, it does not have to be that way after cooking. Families have been eating and enjoying wild game for generations, and as a result, special techniques have been developed for preparing juicy, tender, and superbly flavorful game meat dishes.

Freshwater fish, saltwater fish and shellfish, which include well over 200 varieties, offer more taste diversity to our menus than any other meat. Depending on the season and the location, fresh fish and shellfish are very often the best buy, as well. Frozen and canned fish may seem a little expensive, but the extra ease, protein, and flavor they add to mealtime are certainly worth it. On the other hand, the popular brands of frozen, breaded fish sticks are a rather poor buy, despite their appealing price and convenience. Typically, they are not 100% of the fish they are supposed to be (the figure is probably closer to 50%), and they are often carelessly handled en route from the factory to the supermarket. If fish has a favored place in your menu planning, use the fresh, fresh-frozen, and canned varieties. All of the best recipes are designed for these, your family will enjoy them more, and your money will be spent in the wisest way.

Money and time are always well spent in choosing top-quality meats, the best fish and shellfish, and the most appetizing recipes for family and friends to enjoy. Just because meats are a routine part of wise meal planning does not mean they should be prepared without care and imagination. No two tunes are alike, nor are any two good meat or seafood recipes. The members of high school bands and choral groups love good food as much as they love music, and salute this Medley of Meats Cookbook with a roll of the drums and a fanfare of horns. They are sure you will love it, too.

CALORIE COMPOSITION CHART

BEEF & VEAL (Average Serving)

Beef Barbecue 301
Beef Roast 202
Beef Stew 252
Chuck Roast....................304
Corned Beef 252
Corned Beef Hash, 1/2 cup 153
Beef Steak 203
Rib Roast 303
Beef Short Ribs 204
Beef Stroganoff 352
Filet Mignon 253
Hamburger Patty, 2 oz. 201
Meat Loaf.....................226
Calves Liver 162
Chili Con Carne, 1/2 cup 251
Veal Chop, breaded, 4 oz. 224
Veal Cutlet 127
Veal Scallopini 377

PORK (Average Serving or Slice)

Bacon, 3 crisp strips 104
Bacon, Canadian, 1 1/2 oz. 102
Barbecue Pork Ribs, 6 252
Pork Roast 203
Pork Chop, 1 224
Pork Sausage, two 3" patties 151
Pork Liver 151
Ham, baked 355
Ham, deviled, 1 tbsp. 102
Smoked Ham 452

POULTRY (Average Serving)

Barbecue Chicken.................202
Baked Chicken 201
Fried Chicken, 1/2 medium..........324
Chicken Livers, 1 52
Chicken Pie 350
Chicken Salad 227
Poultry Giblets 152

Turkey, roasted 176
Turkey Hash....................174
Duck, roast, 3 1/2 oz. 232
Roast Goose 174
Pheasant 172
Quail 224

SEAFOOD (Average Serving)

Baked Red Snapper 101
Baked Salmon 252
Codfish Balls 106
Canned Shrimp, 4 oz. 144
Canned Tuna In Oil, 1/4 cup 124
Clams, 12 medium 104
Clams, fried, 6 medium 201
Crab Meat, 1/2 cup 64
Deviled Crab, 1 medium 201
Flounder 152
Fried Oysters, 6 average 252
Fried Perch 202
Seafood Gumbo, 1 cup 123
Haddock 182
Halibut 203
Herring 223
Trout, 1/2 pound 224
Raw Oysters, 12 average 102
Mussels, 12 average 126
Scallops 103
Mackerel 152
Lobster, 1 average 101
Lobster Newburg 353
Lobster Tails 101

LAMB & GAME (Average Serving)

Barbecued Lamb 352
Lamb Chop, 1" thick 253
Rabbit 176
Lamb Stew 253
Rabbit Fricassee 225
Mutton Chops, 1 1/2" thick 124
Hasenpfeffer (Rabbit) 252

Ground Beef A Cappella

Cooking with ground beef is rather like composing successful music, because both should adapt easily to dozens of variations on the same theme. A good melody can be arranged for rock and roll, an orchestra, a marching band, or for vocal groups just as ground beef is suited for casseroles, meat loaves, pies, sandwiches, soups and stews. Adaptable appeal — that is the secret of ground beef's success in modern meal planning. Ground beef is also a star in dollar-stretching economy, as only one pound of ground beef can serve anywhere from 4 to 10 hungry people. Ground beef can be in the limelight at any time — at a typical family dinner or for a special party feast — and you can be confident of a perfect performance every time. Grocery stores may also feature mixtures of ground beef, pork and veal, which gives us yet another variation on one of America's most popular mealtime themes.

With most homemakers, it is a most challenging job to create new and appealing menu arrangements almost every day and still stick to the food budget. If the appeal of your prize meat loaf recipe is beginning to fade, *Meat Loaf Melody* is an excellent change of pace. And, if you have been searching for a truly festive ground beef dish, try *Meatballs in Dill Sauce*. Your home may be the place where hungry teenagers gather on Saturday afternoons . . . if so, your son or daughter can prepare *Stroganoff Burgers* in a snap — with a little help from their friends, of course.

High school musical groups know how well they love any dish that contains ground beef. Their busy mothers, always on the go, love the ease, economy, and convenience of ground beef. The recipes in this section are exactly what you need if you've wanted to use more ground beef in meal planning, but lacked plenty of dependable, delectable ideas. Ground beef has its place at your table, because it will receive rave reviews every time!

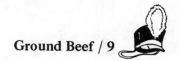

CHAFING DISH DIP

1 lb. hamburger
1/2 onion, chopped
1 clove of garlic, chopped
1 8-oz. can tomato sauce
1/4 c. catsup
3/4 tsp. oregano
1 tbsp. sugar
1 8-oz. package cream cheese,
    softened
1/3 c. grated Parmesan cheese

Cook hamburger and onion until brown. Stir in garlic, tomato sauce, catsup, oregano and sugar; cover. Simmer for 10 minutes; spoon off excess fat. Simmer for 10 minutes longer. Add cheeses; stir until melted. Pour into chafing dish. Serve with tortilla chips or corn chips. Yield: 3 cups.

MEATBALLS IN PEA SOUP

1 1/4 c. split peas
1/4 c. rice
3 med. onions, chopped
1 tsp. thyme
1/2 lb. ground beef
2 beef bouillon cubes
Salt and pepper

Combine peas, rice, 1 cup onions and thyme with 2 quarts water; cook for 1 hour or until peas and rice are tender. Shape beef into small balls; brown in skillet. Remove from skillet; set aside. Cook remaining onion in beef drippings for 10 minutes or until tender. Add meatballs and onion to rice mixture. Add bouillon cubes; stir gently until dissolved. Season to taste.

SPICY SOUP SONATA

1 1/2 lb. ground beef
1 lg. onion, chopped
4 lg. potatoes, cubed
4 carrots, sliced
1/2 head cabbage, shredded
4 c. tomatoes
1/2 bay leaf
1/4 tsp. thyme

Salt and pepper to taste
1/4 c. rice

Saute ground beef and onion in small amount of fat in Dutch oven; drain off fat. Add 4 cups water, potatoes, carrots, cabbage, tomatoes, bay leaf, thyme, salt and pepper. Bring to a boil. Add rice; reduce heat. Simmer, covered, for 2 hours. Add water as needed during first 30 minutes. Yield: 4-5 servings.

TINY PIZZAS

1 can tomato paste
1/2 tsp. salt
1 1/2 tsp. Worcestershire sauce
1/2 tsp. garlic salt
1/4 tsp. Tabasco sauce
1 can biscuits
3/4 lb. ground beef
3/4 c. grated sharp cheese
Oregano

Combine the first 5 ingredients; mix well. Roll or stretch each biscuit to a thin circle, about 4 inches in diameter. Cover each thin circle with a 1/4-inch layer of uncooked ground beef. Spread with tomato paste mixture. Sprinkle with cheese and oregano. Place on an ungreased baking sheet. Bake for 10 minutes at 425 degrees. Serve hot.

STUFFED PICNIC ROLLS

1 lb. hamburger
1 onion, chopped
2 tbsp. fat
1/3 c. catsup
1 tsp. mustard
1 tsp. salt
Dash of pepper
1 tbsp. Worcestershire sauce
1 c. shredded cheese
8 hamburger buns

Saute hamburger and onion in fat in skillet until onion is tender. Combine all ingredients except buns. Split buns; hollow out inside. Fill buns with hamburger mixture; wrap individually in foil. Bake in 350-degree oven until heated through. May be kept frozen for several days. Yield: 8 servings.

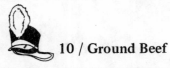

BURGERS IN RAGTIME

1 1/2 lb. lean hamburger
1 c. chopped onion
1 c. chopped celery
1 tsp. salt
Pepper to taste
1 can tomato soup
2 tbsp. barbecue or steak sauce

Brown hamburger meat in skillet over low heat. Add onion and celery. Saute until vegetables are tender. Add remaining ingredients. Simmer, covered, for 20 to 30 minutes. Serve over biscuits or on toast points. Yield: 5 servings.

STROGANOFF BURGERS

2 lb. ground beef
1/3 c. chopped onion
1/3 c. catsup
3 tbsp. prepared mustard
1 tsp. salt
1 12-oz. carton sour cream

Brown ground beef in skillet. Add onion; brown slightly. Add remaining ingredients; mix well. Simmer, covered, for 20 minutes. Serve on heated buns. Yield: 12 servings.

PIZZA POOR BOY

1 1-lb. loaf French bread
1/4 c. chopped ripe olives
1/8 tsp. pepper
1/4 tsp. oregano
Salt to taste
2 tbsp. minced green onion tops
1/2 lb. ground beef
1/4 c. grated Parmesan cheese
1 6-oz. can tomato paste
1/2 lb. process cheese, sliced

Cut loaf in half lengthwise. Combine olives, pepper, oregano, salt, onion tops, ground beef, Parmesan cheese and tomato paste; mix well. Spread over cut sides of bread. Place on baking sheet, spread side up. Bake in 400-degree oven for 15 minutes. Cut cheese slices in half diagonally. Cover ground beef mixture with overlapping triangular slices. Bake for 5 minutes longer. Cut each loaf half into 12 slices.

CHILI CON CARNE

1 med. onion, chopped
1 1/2 lb. lean ground beef
2 tbsp. cooking oil
1 1-lb. can tomatoes
1 8-oz. can seasoned tomato sauce
1 c. catsup
1 1-lb. can kidney beans
1 to 1 1/2 tbsp. chili powder
1 1/2 tsp. salt
1 bay leaf
Dash of ground red pepper

Brown onion and beef in oil in heavy 4-quart saucepan. Add tomatoes, tomato sauce, catsup, beans and seasonings. Simmer, covered, for 1 hour and 30 minutes. Add water if necessary. Yield: 6 servings.

EMPANADAS IMPRESARIO

Paprika to taste
1 lb. ground beef
2 tbsp. chopped onion
Flour
1/2 c. broth
Salt
Pepper
1 hard-cooked egg, chopped
3 tbsp. shortening, melted
1/2 tbsp. vinegar

Blend paprika into beef. Saute in skillet until brown. Add onion. Stir in 1 tablespoon flour and broth; mix well. Cook, stirring constantly, over medium heat until thickened. Season with salt and pepper to taste. Remove from heat; add egg. Measure 4 cups flour into mixing bowl. Season with 1 teaspoon salt. Add 3 tablespoons water, shortening and vinegar, blending well. Knead dough; roll out on floured surface. Cut into 2 1/2-inch rounds. Place spoonfuls of beef mixture on 1 side of rounds. Fold over; seal edges with fork. Fry in deep hot fat until lightly browned.

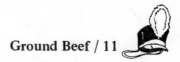

LASAGNA

3/4 lb. ground beef
1/4 lb. bulk sausage
1 sm. onion, minced
1/2 clove of garlic, chopped
1 sm. can mushroom pieces
1 bay leaf, crushed
1 tsp. salt
1/2 tsp. pepper
1 tsp. mixed Italian spices
2 sm. cans tomato paste
1 pkg. lasagna noodles
1 carton ricotta cheese
12 oz. sliced mozzarella cheese
Grated Parmesan cheese

Brown ground beef, sausage and onion in skillet; pour off excess fat. Add garlic, mushroom pieces, seasonings and tomato paste. Rinse each tomato paste can with 3 tablespoons water; stir into meat mixture. Simmer for 45 minutes, stirring occasionally. Cook noodles according to package directions. Alternate layers of noodles, meat sauce, ricotta, mozzarella and Parmesan cheeses in greased oblong baking dish. Repeat layers. Bake in 325-degree oven for 45 minutes.

JOHNNY MARZETTI

1 1/2 lb. ground chuck
2 tbsp. cooking oil
1 bunch celery, chopped
3 green peppers, chopped
6 onions, chopped
1 can tomato soup
1 can tomato paste
1 can tomato sauce
1   4 1/2-oz. bottle stuffed olives,
   sliced
2 cans sliced mushrooms
1 tbsp. Worcestershire sauce
1/4 lb. sharp Cheddar cheese, diced
2 pkg. wide noodles
1/4 lb. grated cheese
1/2 c. bread crumbs
1/2 stick butter

Brown beef in cooking oil; remove to large casserole. Brown celery, peppers and onions in meat drippings; combine vegetables and beef. Add tomato soup, paste and sauce, olives, mushrooms, Worcestershire sauce and diced cheese. Partially cook noodles. Combine noodles with beef and vegetables. Mix well. Mix grated cheese and bread crumbs; spread on top. Dot with butter. Bake at 325 degrees for 1 hour, adding small amount of water if dry. May be made day before except for baking. Freezes well. Yield: 12-15 servings.

QUICHE CHORALE

1/2 lb. ground beef
1/2 c. mayonnaise
1/2 c. milk
2 eggs
1 tbsp. cornstarch
1 1/2 c. diced Cheddar or Swiss cheese
1/3 c. sliced green onions
Dash of pepper
1 unbaked pie shell

Cook beef in skillet over medium heat until brown. Drain off fat; set aside. Blend mayonnaise, milk, eggs and cornstarch until smooth; stir in beef, cheese, onion and pepper. Turn into pie shell. Bake in preheated 350-degree oven for 35 to 40 minutes or until golden brown and knife inserted in center comes out clean. Yield: 6-8 servings.

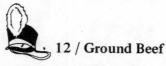

NOODLES MILANESE

1 med. onion, chopped
1 clove of garlic, minced (opt.)
2 tbsp. salad or olive oil
1 lb. ground beef
1 3 or 4-oz. can mushrooms
1 8-oz. can tomato sauce
1 can tomato paste
1 bay leaf
1 tsp. oregano
2 tsp. salt
2 eggs
1 8-oz. package wide noodles, cooked
    and drained
1 pkg. frozen chopped spinach,
    thawed and drained
1/4 c. chopped parsley
1 c. cottage cheese or 1/2 lb.
    cream cheese
1/4 c. grated Parmesan cheese
1 tsp. basil
4 slices American cheese

Brown onion and garlic lightly in 1 tablespoon oil in medium frypan. Add ground beef; cook until brown. Stir in mushrooms and liquid, tomato sauce, tomato paste, bay leaf, oregano and 1 teaspoon salt; simmer 15 minutes. Beat 1 egg in medium bowl. Pour over noodles; mix well. Beat second egg in same bowl; add spinach, 1 tablespoon oil, parsley, cottage cheese, Parmesan cheese, 1 teaspoon salt and basil. Mix well. Pour half the tomato mixture into oblong shallow 8 to 10-cup baking dish. Layer half the noodles on sauce. Spread with spinach-cheese mixture; repeat noodle layer. Top with remaining tomato mixture; cover with lid or foil. Bake in 350-degree oven for 45 minutes. Remove from oven. Arrange strips of American cheese to make squares on top. Bake 5 minutes longer or until cheese is melted. Yield: 6 servings.

ITALIAN SPAGHETTI IN TUNE

2 lb. ground round
2 to 3 tbsp. olive oil
2 sm. cans tomato paste
1 tsp. onion flakes
1 lg. can pear tomatoes
1/2 tomato can water

3 cloves of garlic, chopped
1 tbsp. Italian seasoning
Salt to taste
Cooked spaghetti
1 c. grated Romano cheese

Brown beef in oil in large skillet, stirring to break beef apart. Add remaining ingredients except spaghetti and cheese, mixing well. Cover; simmer for 6 hours, stirring occasionally and adding water as needed. Serve sauce over spaghetti; sprinkle with cheese. Sauce may be frozen. Yield: 8 servings.

TAGLIARINI

1 8-oz. package noodles
1 onion, chopped
1/2 clove of garlic, minced
1 bell pepper, chopped
Cooking oil
1 sm. can tomatoes
2 lb. hamburger
Salt to taste
Dash of red pepper
1 can whole kernel corn
1 can ripe olives and liquid
1/2 lb. Cheddar cheese, grated

Cook noodles according to package directions; drain. Fry onion, garlic and bell pepper in small amount of cooking oil until tender. Add tomatoes; cook for 10 minutes. Add noodles. Brown hamburger with salt and red pepper in 2 tablespoons cooking oil. Add noodle mixture and corn; cook for 10 minutes. Chop ripe olives, reserving 4 or 5 to place on top of casserole. Add chopped olives and half the olive liquid to noodle mixture. Add part of the Cheddar cheese. Pour into casserole. Sprinkle remaining Cheddar cheese on top. Garnish with reserved olives. Bake in 350-degree oven for 1 hour. Yield: 10 servings.

SWEET AND SOUR PATTIES

2 c. bread crumbs
1/4 c. chopped onion
1 tsp. salt
1/8 tsp. thyme

1 lb. ground beef
1 c. sliced onion
1/3 c. (firmly packed) brown sugar
1 tbsp. flour
1/4 c. vinegar
2 tsp. prepared mustard

Combine crumbs, chopped onion, seasonings and 1/2 cup water. Let stand for 5 minutes. Combine ground beef with crumb mixture. Shape into patties. Brown in small amount of hot fat. Cover with sliced onion. Combine brown sugar, flour, vinegar, 2 tablespoons water and mustard. Pour over meat. Simmer, covered, for 35 minutes. Yield: 4-5 servings.

SUPER SALISBURY STEAK

1 c. stale bread crumbs
Milk
1 lb. ground beef
1/2 env. dry onion soup mix or
   1/2 c. chopped onion
1 tbsp. Worcestershire sauce
1 tbsp. salt
2 tbsp. cooking oil
1 can cream of mushroom soup
1 soup can water

Soak bread crumbs in small amount of milk. Mix with ground beef and remaining ingredients except cooking oil, soup and water. Shape into patties. Brown lightly in cooking oil. Add soup and water. Bake at 350 degrees for 30 minutes or until done.

PIZZA MEAT LOAF

1 1/2 lb. ground beef
1 1 1/8-oz. envelope French's Ground Beef
   Seasoning with Onions
1/2 c. fine dry bread crumbs
1 egg, slightly beaten
1/2 c. barbecue sauce, catsup or chili sauce
3 slices process American cheese
1 3-oz. can sliced mushrooms (opt.)

Mix together lightly meat, seasoning mix, bread crumbs, egg and 1/4 cup barbecue sauce. Shape meat mixture into a large flat patty in pizza pan. Broil for 10 minutes. Brush remaining 1/4 cup barbecue sauce over top of meat. Cut cheese slices in half diagonally. Arrange on top of meat in a pie-shaped pattern. Place mushroom slices on each piece of cheese. Return to oven. Broil another 2 minutes or until cheese melts.

Photograph for this recipe on page 8.

MEAT LOAF MELODY

2 lb. ground beef
2 1/2 c. grated American cheese
1 tsp. salt
1/4 tsp. pepper
1 tsp. dry mustard
3 tbsp. catsup
1 tbsp. Worcestershire sauce
2 c. corn flakes
1 c. milk
2 eggs, beaten
Catsup

Combine all ingredients except catsup, mixing well. Press beef mixture into a greased loaf pan. Cut 3 diagonal lines on loaf with sharp knife; fill indentations with catsup. Bake in a preheated 350-degree oven for 1 hour.

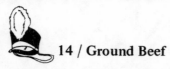

CHORUS LOAVES WITH BORDELAISE SAUCE

1 beaten egg
1/2 c. chopped onion
1/2 c. chopped green pepper
1/2 c. chopped celery
4 crumbled crackers
1 lb. ground beef
Pinch of each salt, pepper and
*   garlic powder*
Bordelaise Sauce

Add egg, onion, green pepper, celery and crackers to beef. Sprinkle with salt, pepper and garlic powder, mixing well. Roll into small individual loaves. Place in shallow baking dish. Bake in 425-degree oven for 30 minutes. Serve with Bordelaise Sauce. May be frozen.

Bordelaise Sauce

1/2 tbsp. chopped green onions
3/4 c. red wine
1/2 bay leaf
Pinch of thyme
1/3 c. sliced fresh mushrooms
2 tbsp. butter
1 tbsp. arrowroot powder
1 c. strained beef broth
Salt and pepper

Simmer onions, wine, bay leaf and thyme until wine is reduced to 1/4 cup; strain. Saute mushrooms in butter; stir in arrowroot powder and broth. Stir until mixture boils thoroughly and becomes clear. Add salt and pepper to taste; add wine mixture. Simmer for 5 minutes. Yield: 6-8 servings.

MEAT LOAF AND POTATOES IN HARMONY

2 lb. ground chuck
1/2 c. herb-seasoned stuffing mix
1/2 c. tomato juice
1 tsp. salt
1 2-oz. can sliced mushrooms
1 tsp. dried parsley flakes
6 med. peeled potatoes, quartered
Garlic salt
Parmesan cheese

Combine first 6 ingredients; mix well. Shape into loaf. Place in 13 x 9 x 2-inch Pyrex baking dish. Place potatoes around loaf. Sprinkle generously with garlic salt and cheese. Bake at 350 degrees for 1 hour, basting potatoes once or twice. Yield: 8-10 servings.

SPICY MEAT LOAF

2 lb. hamburger
2 eggs
2 c. Special K cereal
1 can onion soup
Salt and pepper to taste

Mix all ingredients together. Shape into loaf. Place in shallow pan. Bake at 350 degrees about 1 hour. Yield: 10 servings.

MEAT LOAF OVERTURE

2 eggs
1 1/2 c. soft bread crumbs
1/4 tsp. pepper
2 tsp. salt
1 tsp. Worcestershire sauce
3/4 c. milk
1/2 c. chopped onion
1 c. chopped carrots
2 lb. ground beef

Beat eggs; stir in crumbs, seasonings, milk and vegetables. Add ground beef. Shape into 2 loaves. Place in 7 x 4 x 2-inch loaf pans. Bake at 350 degrees for 1 hour. Yield: 10-12 servings.

APPLESAUCE MEATBALLS

2 lb. ground beef
1 egg, beaten
1 c. rolled oats
1 onion, chopped
1/2 tsp. salt
Pinch of pepper
1/4 tsp. garlic salt
1/2 c. applesauce
1 6-oz. can tomato sauce

Mix all ingredients except tomato sauce; shape into balls. Place in roasting pan in single layer; pour tomato sauce over meatballs. Cover. Bake in pre-heated 350-degree oven for 1 hour. Uncover; bake for 30 minutes longer.

GOURMET MEATBALLS

2 lb. ground beef
1   12-oz. bottle chili sauce
1   16-oz. can jellied cranberry sauce
1   10 3/4-oz. can tomato soup

Shape beef into small balls. Brown in skillet. Drain off grease. Combine remaining ingredients. Pour over meatballs. Bake at 250 degrees for 2 hours. Yield: 4-6 servings.

MEATBALLS IN DILL SAUCE

2 lb. ground beef
2 med. onions, ground
1 egg
1 tsp. salt
1/4 tsp. pepper
1/2 tsp. Italian seasoning
Cracker meal
1 can mushroom soup
1 pt. fresh mushrooms, sliced
1 c. sour cream
1/2 c. dry white wine
2 sprigs of dill, chopped

Combine beef, onions, egg and seasonings; shape into small balls. Dip balls in cracker meal; brown in skillet in small amount of hot fat. Place in 2-quart baking dish. Blend soup with mushrooms, 2/3 cup sour cream and wine. Bake at 350 degrees for 30 minutes. Remove from oven; spoon remaining sour cream and dill over top. Yield: 8 servings.

SAUERBRATEN MEATBALLS

1 lb. ground beef
1/4 c. fine dry bread crumbs
2/3 c. chopped onions
1 1/2 tsp. salt
Dash of pepper

2/3 c. evaporated milk
2 tbsp. butter
1 c. water
2 tbsp. vinegar
2 tbsp. catsup
1 tbsp. (packed) brown sugar
8 peppercorns, crushed
1 bay leaf, crumbled
1/3 c. raisins
6 gingersnaps, crushed

Combine beef, bread crumbs, onions, 1 teaspoon salt, pepper and milk; shape into balls. Brown meatballs in skillet in butter. Combine remaining ingredients with 1 cup water; mix well. Pour sauce over meatballs. Bring to a boil over medium heat; reduce heat. Simmer, covered, for 15 minutes. Stir gently. Simmer, covered, for 15 minutes longer. Yield: 6 servings.

SWEET AND SOUR MEATBALLS

1 sm. jar grape jelly
1   12-oz. jar chili sauce
1 lb. hamburger

Melt grape jelly in chili sauce. Form hamburger into small balls with wet hands. Drop into jelly mixture. Cook over low heat, uncovered, for 20 minutes. May be served over rice as main course.

SWEDISH MEATBALLS

2 cans consomme
10 gingersnaps, crushed
4 tsp. brown sugar
1 1/2 tsp. lemon juice
3 lb. ground beef
Parsley to taste
Chopped onion to taste
1/2 c. bread crumbs
2 eggs
Salt and pepper to taste
1 sm. potato, grated

Combine first 4 ingredients in saucepan; simmer for 15 minutes. Combine remaining ingredients. Shape into small balls. Drop into sauce. Cook meatballs for 30 minutes. Yield: 20 servings.

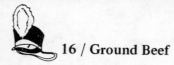
SCALLOPED MEATBALLS AND POTATOES

4 c. thinly sliced potatoes
4 tbsp. butter
4 tbsp. flour
2 c. milk
1 c. water
2 tsp. salt
Dash of pepper
1 lb. ground beef
3 tbsp. chili sauce
1 1/4 tsp. prepared mustard
1 1/4 tsp. bottled horseradish
1 1/2 tsp. grated onion
1 1/4 tsp. Worcestershire sauce

Cook potatoes in salted water for 10 minutes. Drain; arrange in baking dish. Melt butter in saucepan. Stir in flour; add milk and water, stirring until thickened. Add 1 teaspoon salt and small amount of pepper. Pour over potatoes. Combine remaining ingredients. Shape into 10 balls. Place meatballs over potatoes. Bake, uncovered, at 350 degrees for 45 minutes or until done. Yield: 6 servings.

MEXICAN MARACAS

1 lb. ground beef
1 sm. onion, chopped
1 green pepper, chopped
4 lg. stalks celery, chopped
2 tbsp. flour
3/4 c. catsup
2 tbsp. chili powder
Salt to taste
1 lg. bag corn chips
1/2 lb. grated Cheddar cheese
1 sm. can chopped olives
1 avocado, peeled and sliced
2 c. shredded lettuce
3 tomatoes, chopped

Crumble beef into large skillet; brown over medium heat. Drain off excess fat. Add 1/2 cup water, onion, green pepper and celery. Mix flour with small amount of water, stirring until blended. Add to beef mixture, stirring constantly, until thickened. Stir in catsup. Add chili powder and salt; stir well. Simmer until celery is tender. Spoon onto plates over layer of corn chips. Sprinkle cheese over top; allow cheese to melt.

Top with spoonfuls of chopped olives, avocado, lettuce and tomatoes. Yield: 4 servings.

ENCHILADA PIE

1 lb. ground beef
1 c. chopped onions
1 clove of garlic, minced
2 tbsp. butter
1 tsp. salt
1/4 tsp. pepper
1 tbsp. chili powder
1   4 1/2-oz. can chopped black olives
1   8-oz. can tomato sauce
6 corn tortillas, buttered
2 c. grated Cheddar cheese
2/3 c. water

Saute ground beef, onions and garlic in butter until lightly browned. Add seasonings, olives and tomato sauce. Place alternate layers of tortillas, beef sauce and cheese in round 2-quart casserole, ending with cheese. Pour water, at edge, into casserole; cover. Bake in preheated 400-degree oven for 30 minutes; cut into wedges. Yield: 4 generous servings.

B-SHARP BEEF AND DUMPLINGS

1 lb. ground beef
1 sm. onion, chopped
1   8-oz. package dumplings
3 c. tomato juice
2 tsp. salt
Dash of pepper
2 tsp. Worcestershire sauce
1 c. sour cream
Grated Parmesan cheese to taste
Paprika to taste

Brown ground beef and onion in 2 tablespoons hot fat in heavy saucepan. Place dumplings in layer over ground beef mixture. Mix remaining ingredients except sour cream, cheese and paprika. Pour over dumplings. Bring to a boil. Simmer, covered, for 40 minutes or until dumplings are tender. Stir in sour cream. Bring to a boil. Remove from heat immediately. Turn into serving dish. Sprinkle with cheese and paprika. Yield: 4 servings.

Recipe for this photograph on page 25.

MEXICAN-STYLE ENCHILADA CASSEROLE

2 lb. hamburger
1 lg. onion, chopped
1 can cream of mushroom soup
1 can cream of chicken soup
1 can mild or hot enchilada sauce
1 can green chilies, diced
1 c. milk
Salt and garlic salt to taste
Paprika to taste
2 doz. soft tortillas

Cook hamburger in large, heavy pot until brown. Drain in colander; reserve several tablespoons fat. Pour reserved fat into same pot. Add onion; saute until tender. Add hamburger, mushroom soup, chicken soup, enchilada sauce, green chilies and milk. Cook over low heat, stirring, until heated through. Season with salt, garlic salt and paprika. Place layer of tortillas in casserole; cover with layer of beef mixture. Repeat layers until all ingredients are used. Bake, covered, in preheated 350-degree oven for 45 minutes. Freezes well.

SHEPHERD'S PIE

1 lb. hamburger
Salt
Pepper to taste
1 tbsp. oil
4 or 5 med. potatoes, cooked
3 tbsp. butter
1/4 c. milk
1 can whole kernel or cream-style corn

Cook hamburger, 1/2 teaspoon salt and pepper in oil until hamburger is brown. Mash potatoes with butter, milk, salt to taste and pepper. Place alternate layers of hamburger, potatoes and corn in 1 1/2-quart casserole, ending with potatoes. May sprinkle top with cheese and dot with butter, if desired. Bake in preheated 350-degree oven for 30 minutes.

SKILLET LUAU

1 lb. ground beef
1 egg, beaten

Recipes for this photograph on page 28.

1/4 c. dry bread crumbs
1/2 tsp. salt
1/4 tsp. ginger
1/4 c. flour
1 No. 2 can pineapple chunks
3 tbsp. (packed) brown sugar
3/4 tsp. cornstarch
1/4 c. vinegar
1 tbsp. soy sauce
2 green peppers, cut into strips

Mix beef with egg, crumbs, salt and ginger; form into 16 balls. Dredge balls in flour; brown in 3 tablespoons fat in large frypan. Remove meatballs from pan. Drain pineapple, reserving syrup. Add water to syrup to make 1 cup liquid. Stir syrup mixture into pan drippings. Mix brown sugar with cornstarch, vinegar and soy sauce. Add to syrup mixture. Cook, stirring constantly, until sauce is thickened and clear. Arrange meatballs, pineapple chunks and pepper strips separately in pan. Stir each gently to coat with sauce. Simmer, covered, for 10 minutes or until green pepper is crisp-tender. Serve with hot buttered noodles, if desired. Yield: 4 servings.

GROUND BEEF AND ZUCCHINI DUO

6 med. zucchini
1 lb. ground beef
1 med. onion, chopped
1 No. 2 1/2 can tomatoes
1 8-oz. can tomato sauce
1 6-oz. can tomato paste
1 sm. green pepper, chopped
1 c. grated sharp Cheddar cheese
1/2 c. pitted ripe olives
1/2 tsp. salt
1/4 tsp. garlic salt
1/8 tsp. oregano
Grated Parmesan cheese

Cut zucchini into 1/2-inch slices. Saute beef and onion in 1 tablespoon fat in large skillet. Add zucchini, tomatoes, tomato sauce, tomato paste, green pepper, Cheddar cheese, olives, salt, garlic salt and oregano. Simmer for 10 minutes. Place in 8 x 12-inch pan. Sprinkle with Parmesan cheese generously. Bake at 350 degrees for 1 hour or until thickened and browned. Yield: 8 servings.

GERSHWIN'S PARTY PLEASER

2 lg. onions, chopped
1 lb. fresh mushrooms, sliced
2 tbsp. margarine
1 1/2 lb. ground round steak
1 No. 2 can tomatoes
1/2 tsp. basil
1/2 tsp. oregano
1/2 tsp. pepper
1/2 tsp. garlic salt
5 drops of hot sauce
Salt to taste
1 c. spaghetti rings
1/2 pkg. herb-seasoned stuffing mix
1/2 c. grated Parmesan cheese
1 No. 303 can zucchini

Saute onions and mushrooms in margarine in large pan. Add ground steak; cook, stirring occasionally, until slightly browned. Lower heat; add remaining ingredients. Stir, mixing well. Turn into casserole. Bake at 325 degrees for 45 minutes, adding water as needed. Yield: 4-5 servings.

HAMBURGER QUICKIE

Salt and pepper to taste
1 lb. hamburger
1 sm. bottle olives
1 med. onion, chopped
Catsup to taste

Add salt and pepper to hamburger; cook until well done. Press out grease on paper towels; place in bowl. Add olives, onion and catsup; mix and serve. Yield: 4 servings.

STUFFED GREEN PEPPERS

1 lb. ground beef
1 c. rice
1 sm. onion, minced
1 egg
Salt and pepper to taste
4 green peppers
1 lg. can tomato puree

Mix ground beef, rice, onion, egg, salt and pepper. Remove stem ends of green peppers; fill peppers with beef mixture. Shape remaining beef mixture into balls; place green peppers and meatballs in saucepan. Add tomato puree and 1 tomato puree can water. Simmer for about 1 hour or until beef mixture is done, adding water, if needed.

SOUTHERN STUFFED PEPPERS

8 lg. green peppers
1/4 c. chopped onion
2 tbsp. cooking oil
1 lb. ground beef
1 1/2 c. cooked rice
1/2 c. grated cheese
1 c. canned tomatoes
1 1/2 tsp. Worcestershire sauce
1/4 tsp. paprika
1/2 tsp. celery salt
1/4 tsp. salt
1/2 c. lightly browned bread crumbs

Remove tops and centers from peppers. Parboil in boiling water for 12 minutes. Saute onion in cooking oil. Add beef and brown. Combine all ingredients except crumbs and peppers. Stuff peppers with mixture. Stand upright in greased baking dish. Sprinkle with buttered bread crumbs. Bake at 350 degrees for 25 minutes. Water may be added during baking period if needed. Yield: 6-8 servings.

PICKLE AND BEEF-STUFFED TOMATOES

4 lg. tomatoes
Salt
2 tbsp. butter or margarine
2 tbsp. chopped onion
1/2 lb. ground chuck
1/8 tsp. basil
1/2 c. bread crumbs
1/3 c. chopped sweet pickles
2 tbsp. grated Parmesan cheese

Cut slice from stem end of each tomato; scoop out pulp, leaving outside wall about 1/4 inch thick. Reserve 1/2 cup tomato pulp. Sprinkle inside of tomatoes with salt. Melt butter. Add onion and chuck; cook until chuck is brown. Add 1/2 teaspoon salt, basil, bread crumbs and pickles. Add reserved tomato pulp; mix well. Fill tomato shells with beef mixture; top with cheese. Place in shallow baking dish; add enough water to fill dish 1/4 inch full. Bake in preheated 350-degree oven for 35 minutes or until tomatoes are tender.

CABBAGE ROLLS WITH RAISINS

1 1/2 c. raisins
1 lb. ground beef
1 c. rice, cooked
1 onion, chopped
2 tsp. salt
1/2 tsp. turmeric
Cabbage leaves
1 can beef broth
1/4 c. catsup
1 tbsp. vinegar
1 tbsp. cornstarch

Combine 1 cup raisins with beef, rice, onion, salt, turmeric and 1/4 cup water. Cover cabbage leaves with hot water; simmer for just 2 minutes. Drain; trim off thick portions from base of leaves. Spoon beef filling onto center of leaves; fold in sides. Roll up leaves; secure with toothpicks. Place in heavy pan; add beef broth. Simmer, covered, for 30 minutes. Remove cabbage rolls; keep warm. Add enough water to liquid in pan to make 3/4 cup liquid. Add catsup, vinegar, cornstarch and remaining raisins. Cook, stirring, until clear. Return cabbage rolls; cook for 5 minutes longer.

Beef And Veal Variations

For a virtuoso dinner performance that Beethoven himself would applaud, offer beef or veal dishes as an enlivening entree for any family or party menu. Although they come from the same animal, beef and veal are as different from one another as a majestic anthem is from a blues melody. Roasts, steaks, and other cuts of beef have a robust flavor and a juicy, hearty texture, while the flavor of veal is light, delicate, and slightly dry. Beef is always a good choice because it is satisfying enough for hungry, active family members, economical enough for the family budget, as well as elegant and festive enough for all special occasions. Veal is one of the favorite meats of Italians, people who cook and dine with a flair. Veal has little natural fats and juices, so it is the perfect meat for a superb sauce. However, veal also tends to pick up the flavors of the foods it is cooked and served with. So, enhancing side dishes and sauces are the best choice of accompaniments. Prepared thoughtfully, veal can be a dish that anyone would term *vivace!*

As impressario of the dinner table, you never settle for anything less than the best. On that note, you'll be proud to serve *Drummer's Dumplings and Round Steak, Corned Beef Pie Allegro,* or *Marinated Roast Beef.* Maybe your budget currently demands supper for a song? Then try *Braised Short Ribs* for an economical beef fanfare. For an entree featuring veal in an unforgettable arrangement, serve *Lemon Veal Supreme,* and as an encore, *Veal Ragout Mancini.*

Beef has become an integral part of American mealtimes because it is a palate-pleasing food *par excellence,* and quite healthful, as well. Veal is equally nutritious, and more and more homemakers are discovering its taste appeal every day. Generation-proven recipes have been developed for both, and high school choir and band members believe the recipes they offer in this section are some of the best. Use veal more often in your meal planning, and don't hesitate to serve beef as often as you please.

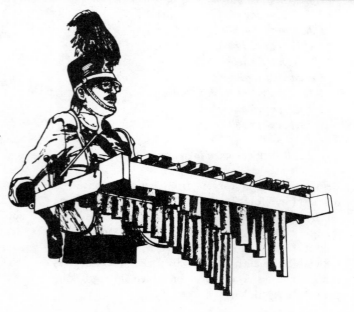

RETAIL BEEF CUTS AND HOW TO COOK THEM

Inside Chuck Roll · Chuck Short Ribs · Chuck Tender · Petite Steaks* · Blade Pot roast or Steak · Arm Pot roast or Steak · Boneless Shoulder Pot roast or Steak · Boston Cut

CHUCK — Braise, Cook in Liquid

Standing Rib Roast · Rib Steak · Rib Steak, Boneless · Delmonico (Rib Eye) Roast or Steak

RIB — Roast, Broil, Panbroil, Panfry

Club Steak · T-Bone Steak · Porterhouse Steak · Top Loin Steak · Filet Mignon Tenderloin Steak (also from Sirloin 1, 2, 3)

SHORT LOIN — Roast, Broil, Panbroil, Panfry

Pin Bone Sirloin Steak · Flat Bone Sirloin Steak · Wedge Bone Sirloin Steak · Boneless Sirloin Steak

SIRLOIN — Roast, Broil, Panbroil, Panfry

Round Steak · Standing Rump* · Top Round Steak* · Rolled Rump* · Outside (Bottom) Round Steak or Pot roast · Eye of Round · Heel of Round

ROUND — Braise, Cook in Liquid

Shank Cross Cuts · Beef for Stew (also from other cuts)

FORE SHANK — Braise, Cook in Liquid

Fresh Brisket · Corned Brisket

BRISKET — Braise, Cook in Liquid

Short Ribs · Skirt Steak Fillets* · Rolled Plate · Plate Beef

SHORT PLATE — Braise, Cook in Liquid

Ground Beef (Flank, Short Plate, Shank, Brisket, Rib, Chuck, Loin, Round) · Beef Patties

GROUND BEEF — Roast, Broil, Panbroil, Panfry

Flank Steak* · Flank Steak Fillets*

FLANK STEAK — Braise, Cook in Liquid

Tip Steak* · Sirloin Tip* · Cube Steak*

TIP (KNUCKLE) — Braise, Cook in Liquid

* May be Roasted, Broiled, Panbroiled or Panfried from high quality beef.

TIMETABLE FOR COOKING BEEF

CUT	ROASTED AT 300 F. OVEN TEMPERATURE		BROILED		BRAISED	COOKED IN LIQUID
	Meat Thermometer Reading Degrees F.	Time Minutes per lb.	Meat Thermometer Reading Degrees F.	Total Time Minutes	Total Time Hours	Total Time Hours
Standing Ribs	140 (rare)	18 to 20				
Standing Ribs	160 (medium)	22 to 25				
Standing Ribs	170 (well)	27 to 30				
Rolled Ribs	Same as above	Add 10 to 15				
Blade, 3rd to 5th Rib (high quality only)	150-170	25 to 30				
Rump (high quality only)	150-170	25 to 30				
Tenderloin	140-170	20 to 25				
Beef Loaf	160-170	25 to 30				
Steaks (1 inch)			140 (rare) 160 (medium)	15 to 20 20 to 30		
Steaks (1 1/2 inch)			140 (rare) 160 (medium)	25 to 35 35 to 50		
Steaks (2 inch)			140 (rare) 160 (medium)	30 to 40 50 to 70		
Beef Patties (1 inch)			140 (rare) 160 (medium)	12 to 15 18 to 20		
Pot-Roasts						
Arm or Blade					3 to 4	
Rump					3 to 4	
Swiss Steak					2 to 3	
Corned Beef						3 1/2 to 5
Fresh Beef					3 to 4	3 to 4
Stew						2 to 3

DANISH SANDWICHES

Mermaid's Medley

4 or 5 rare or med. slices roast beef
Lettuce
3 spears asparagus
Hard-cooked egg yolks, sieved
Capers to taste
Radishes to taste

Arrange roast beef on lettuce bed. Top with asparagus. Garnish with egg yolks, capers and radishes.

Jutland Jubilee

1 tbsp. horseradish
3 tbsp. cream cheese
3 slices chopped ham or luncheon meat
Lettuce
3 thin apple wedges coated with
*   lemon juice*

Blend horseradish and cream cheese. Spread mixture on ham slices; roll into ham rolls. Alternate on lettuce with apple wedges. Garnish with mayonnaise and chopped nuts.

Copenhagen Cloverleaf

Salami slices
Lettuce
Cucumber slices
Hard-cooked eggs

Place 2 to 4 slices of salami flat on lettuce. Arrange 3 folded slices of salami in cloverleaf pattern on top. Top each with cucumber slices and eggs. Garnish with pimento and parsley.

Royal Roast Beef

3 to 5 slices rare or med. roast beef
Lettuce
3 bacon curls
1 recipe egg salad

Place roast beef slices on lettuce. Arrange bacon curls in diagonal row across top. Place 1 tablespoon egg salad in each space between curls. Garnish with tomato wedges and green pepper.

Fairyland Fantasy

3 to 4 slices boiled ham
Lettuce
2 cooked prunes
Cream cheese
Orange slices

Arrange ham slices on lettuce, folding and overlapping slices. Stuff prunes with cream cheese. Top ham with prunes, alternating with thin twisted orange slices.

Tivoli Tempter

Bread slices
Liver sausage
Chopped parsley
3 onion rings
3 mushroom slices

Spread bread with thick layer of liver sausage. Garnish with chopped parsley. Arrange onion rings and mushroom slices diagonally across top. Garnish with bacon curls and cherry tomato stuffed with cream cheese.

Danish Lunch

4 cooked pork slices
Lettuce
1 recipe potato salad
2 green pepper rings

Arrange 2 pork slices on lettuce. Top with 2 diagonally folded slices, pointing in opposite directions. Place 2 tablespoons potato salad in center; slip 2 green pepper rings under folds of top slices of pork. Garnish as desired.

Photograph for these recipes on the cover.

HEARTY WINTER SOUP

3 1/2 to 4 lb. arm roast, bone in
Salt and pepper to taste
1 soupbone
4 qt. cold water
1 med. Spanish onion, diced
1 1/2 c. diced carrots
1 c. diced celery

1 c. shredded cabbage
1 c. diced potatoes
2 lg. fresh or 1 No. 2 can tomatoes
1/4 tsp. parsley flakes
1 tbsp. Worcestershire sauce

Cut meat into 1/2-inch square pieces. Season with salt and pepper. Brown, adding fat if needed. Add soupbone and water. Bring to a boil slowly. Simmer for 3 hours. Skim fat off surface. Add onion; continue to simmer 15 minutes. Add remaining ingredients. Cook until vegetables are tender. One 1-quart 14-ounce can V-8 juice may be substituted for parsley, tomatoes and Worcestershire sauce. Leftover meat may be added with vegetables and leftover vegetables may be added when carrots are done. Yield: 8-12 servings.

TUNEFUL BEEF SPREAD

Cooked roast beef
1/2 c. nuts
1/2 c. pickle relish
Mayonnaise

Grind roast and nuts together. Add pickle relish and enough mayonnaise to moisten and hold ingredients together. Mix well. Keeps well; may be frozen.

ROCK AND ROLL REUBEN SANDWICH

2 c. drained sauerkraut
1/2 tsp. caraway seed or dillseed
1/8 tsp. garlic powder
16 slices round bread
1/2 c. Russian dressing
1 lb. thinly sliced corned beef
1 lb. Swiss cheese slices
Melted butter or margarine

Toss sauerkraut with caraway seed and garlic powder; set aside. Spread bread with Russian dressing. Top 8 slices bread with corned beef, sauerkraut, cheese and remaining 8 slices bread. Brush melted butter on both sides of sandwiches. Grill in skillet or electric sandwich toaster until cheese is melted.

CORNED BEEF PIE ALLEGRO

1 can corned beef hash
1 c. chopped onions

3 tbsp. butter
3 eggs, slightly beaten
1 c. sour cream
1/2 c. milk
1/8 tsp. pepper
1/2 tsp. salt
1 c. shredded Cheddar cheese

Press hash onto bottom and side of 10-inch pie plate. Cook onions in butter until tender but not brown; spread over hash. Mix eggs, sour cream, milk and seasonings; pour over onions in hash shell. Sprinkle with cheese. Bake at 350 degrees for 35 to 40 minutes or until set. Yield: 6 servings.

CLASSIC TEXAS CHILI

1/4 c. salad oil
3 lb. beef stew meat, cut in 1-in. cubes
3 cloves of garlic, minced
4 to 6 tbsp. chili powder
2 tsp. salt
2 tsp. dried leaf oregano
2 tsp. ground cumin
2 tsp. Tabasco pepper sauce
1 1/2 qt. water
1/3 c. white cornmeal

Heat oil in large saucepan or kettle. Add beef; brown on all sides. Add garlic, chili powder, salt, oregano, cumin, Tabasco and water. Stir to mix well. Bring to a boil. Cover and reduce heat. Simmer for 1 hour and 15 minutes, stirring occasionally. Add cornmeal; mix well. Simmer, uncovered, for an additional 30 minutes or until meat is tender. Garnish with chopped onion. Serve with rice and beans. Yield: 6-8 servings.

Photograph for this recipe on page 17.

BRAISED SHORT RIBS

3 lb. beef short ribs
Salt
3/4 c. long grain rice
1/2 c. chopped onion
1/2 c. chopped celery
1/4 c. chopped green pepper
2 1/4 c. water
2 tsp. beef gravy base
1 tsp. Worcestershire sauce
1/4 tsp. crushed thyme
1/8 tsp. pepper

Cut ribs into serving pieces. Brown, without added fat, on all sides in heavy skillet for about 25 to 30 minutes. Season with small amount of salt. Transfer to 3-quart casserole. Bake, covered, at 325 degrees for 1 hour. Combine rice, onion, celery, 2 tablespoons salt and green pepper in skillet in which ribs were browned; mix well. Cook until rice is lightly browned. Remove ribs from casserole; pour off fat. Spread rice mixture in casserole; top with ribs. Combine remaining ingredients in small saucepan; heat to boiling point. Pour over ribs. Bake, covered, for 1 hour longer. Yield: 4-6 servings.

ROLLED RIB ROAST

1 5-lb. rolled rib roast
Salt
Pepper

Season roast with salt and pepper to taste. Place, fat side up, on rack in shallow pan. Insert meat thermometer in center of roast. Bake in 325-degree oven for about 2 hours or to 150 degrees on meat thermometer. Let roast stand for 20 minutes in warm place before carving. Serve with browned whole potatoes. Yield: 12 servings.

Photograph for this recipe on page 22.

KEYNOTE ROAST BEEF

1 3 to 5-lb. roast
1/2 pkg. dry onion soup mix
1/2 pkg. dry mushroom soup mix
4 tbsp. water or mushroom liquid
1 1-oz. can mushrooms, drained

Place roast on large piece of heavy-duty foil. Mix onion and mushroom soup mixes together; sprinkle over roast. Drizzle water over mixes. Sprinkle mushrooms over top. Seal foil tightly. Place roast on cookie sheet. Bake in 250-degree oven for 5 hours or longer. Serve with gravy. One can mushroom soup may be substituted for mushroom soup mix; omit water. Yield: 6-8 servings.

MARINATED ROAST BEEF

1/3 c. vinegar
2 tbsp. salad oil
1/8 tsp. pepper
1/4 tsp. mustard
1/4 tsp. salt
1 tbsp. Worcestershire sauce
4 tsp. sugar
1 med. onion, thinly sliced
1 lb. cooked 1/8-in. thick roast beef
*   slices*
Parsley

Combine vinegar, salad oil, pepper, mustard, salt, Worcestershire sauce, sugar and onion. Marinate beef slices in vinegar mixture for about 3 hours in refrigerator. Remove beef slices and onion from marinade. Serve on cold meat platter. Garnish with parsley. Yield: 6 servings.

DILL POT ROAST WITH CARROT GRAVY

1/4 c. plus 2 tbsp. all-purpose flour
Salt and pepper to taste
1   3 to 4-lb. pot roast
3 tbsp. bacon drippings
1 med. onion, sliced
1 tsp. dillweed
2 tbsp. vinegar
1 c. water
1 c. coarsely grated carrots

Season 1/4 cup flour with salt and pepper. Dredge roast in flour mixture. Brown in bacon drippings. Pour off bacon drippings. Add onion, dillweed, vinegar and 1/2 cup water; cover. Simmer slowly for 2 hours. Add carrots; cook for 1 hour longer or until roast is tender. Remove roast to heated platter. Combine remaining flour with remaining water. Add to pan juices; cook until thickened. Pour gravy over roast. Yield: 6-8 servings.

STEAK DOWN BEAT

1 T-bone steak, 1 1/2 to 2 in. thick
Salt to taste

Let steak stand at room temperature. Preheat oven and broiling pan. Sprinkle steak with salt. Place on rack about 3 inches from source of heat. Broil until brown, turning once. Add salt to other side. Serve on heated platter immediately.

SCINTILLATING STEAK SUZETTE

1   3-lb. sirloin steak
1 tbsp. cracked pepper
1/4 lb. butter
Salt to taste
1 c. dry white wine
1/4 c. brandy
1 tbsp. chopped parsley

Trim fat from steak; cut into 12 uniform pieces. Cover board with heavy waxed paper; lay steak on paper. Sprinkle with pepper; cover with waxed paper. Pound with wooden mallet until 3/8 inch thick. Melt half the butter in hot iron frypan. Sear steak quickly on both sides. Reduce heat; cook for 1 to 4 minutes. Place steak on large hot platter; sprinkle with salt. Add wine to brown residue in pan. Cook rapidly, stirring with wooden spoon, until of syrupy consistency. Remove from heat; stir in remaining butter. Pour heated brandy over steak; light. Allow flames to subside, ladling brandy over steak with spoon. Pour gravy from pan over steak. Sprinkle with parsley; serve at once. Yield: 6-8 servings.

STEAK DIANE

1 tbsp. chopped shallots
3 tbsp. butter
1/2 c. sliced mushrooms
2 New York-cut sirloin steaks
Salt and pepper to taste
1 tbsp. chives
3 tbsp. steak sauce
1 tsp. Worcestershire sauce
1 tsp. mustard

Saute shallots in 2 tablespoons butter until golden brown. Add mushrooms, heating well. Pound sirloins to about 1/2-inch thickness. Season with salt and pepper. Sear on both sides in skillet; move to side of skillet. Add remaining butter, chives, steak sauce, Worcestershire sauce, mushroom mixture and mustard; blend gravy well. Return steaks to center of skillet; simmer until tender. Serve on rice with gravy. Garnish with chopped parsley.

BAKED TENDERLOIN UP BEAT

1 lb. fresh mushrooms, sliced
2 tbsp. butter
1 1/2 tbsp. flour
1/4 tsp. salt
1/8 tsp. pepper
1 tsp. beef extract
1 beef tenderloin

Saute mushrooms in butter. Add flour, salt and pepper; stir until blended. Add 1 cup water and beef extract; cook, stirring, until thickened. Place tenderloin in broiler pan. Broil for 10 minutes. Bake at 375 to 400 degrees for 30 to 40 minutes or to desired degree of doneness. Baste with mushroom sauce. Serve with remaining mushroom sauce. Yield: 8 servings.

IMPERIAL TENDERLOIN ENCORE

1   4 to 6-lb. beef tenderloin
3/4 c. melted butter
1 clove of garlic
1 tbsp. Worcestershire sauce
1/4 lb. bleu cheese

Trim fat from tenderloin. Brush with 1/4 cup butter. Bake on rack at 450 degrees for approximately 45 minutes to 1 hour or until meat thermometer registers 140 degrees. Mash garlic in Worcestershire sauce; combine with bleu cheese and remaining butter. Remove tenderloin from oven. Spread cheese mixture over top. Serve immediately. Yield: 6 servings.

STUFFED BEEFSTEAK QUARTET

1   2-lb. 2-in. thick round steak
Salt and pepper to taste
1 pkg. herb-seasoned stuffing mix
Butter

Season steak with salt and pepper. Prepare stuffing mix according to package directions. Spread over steak. Fold together; seal edges together with skewers. Place in baking pan; dot steak with butter. Add small amount of water to pan. Bake, covered, at 350 degrees for 30 minutes. Uncover. Bake for 30 minutes longer or until tender, basting occasionally with pan juices. Yield: 4 servings.

DOUBLES DELIGHT

Basic Beef Mixture

1/4 c. all-purpose flour
1/2 tsp. salt
1 1/2 lb. trimmed round steak, cut
*   into 3/4 x 1/2 x 2-in. strips*
1/4 c. butter
1/2 lb. fresh mushrooms, sliced
2 tbsp. instant minced onion
1   10 1/2-oz. can beef broth

Combine 2 tablespoons flour and salt; coat meat with mixture. Melt butter in skillet. Brown meat on all sides; cover. Simmer until fork-tender. Remove meat.

Add mushrooms and onion; saute. Return meat to skillet. Sprinkle remaining 2 tablespoons flour over meat; stir to blend. Add beef broth gradually. Cook over medium heat, stirring constantly until thickened. Reduce heat; simmer 3 minutes. Use as directed in recipes where specified.

Biscuit-Topped Stew

1 c. cooked peas and carrots
1/2 recipe Basic Beef Mixture
1 c. buttermilk biscuit mix
1/2 c. shredded Cheddar cheese
1/4 c. milk

Add vegetables to beef mixture. Transfer to 1-quart casserole. Toss together biscuit mix and cheese in a small bowl. Add milk; combine with fork just until blended. Form into ball. Roll on lightly floured surface to 1/2-inch thickness. Cut with 2-inch biscuit cutter. Cut each circle in half. Arrange 10 semicircles around edge of casserole. Place in preheated 450-degree oven for 8 to 10 minutes or until biscuits are golden brown.

Beef Stroganoff

1/2 recipe Basic Beef Mixture
1/2 c. sour cream
1/8 tsp. garlic powder

Heat beef mixture to boiling in large covered skillet. Remove from heat. Stir in sour cream and garlic powder. Heat, uncovered, to serving temperature. Do not boil. Serve over hot buttered noodles. Yield: 2 1/2 cups.

Beef Creole

3/4 c. plain yogurt
1   6-oz. can tomato paste
1/2 recipe Basic Beef Mixture
1/2 med. green pepper, cut into julienne
*   strips*

Blend yogurt and tomato paste in small bowl. Heat beef mixture to boiling in large covered skillet. Remove from heat. Stir in yogurt mixture and green pepper. Heat, uncovered, to serving temperature. Do not boil. Serve over hot buttered rice. Yield: 3 cups.

Photograph for this recipe on page 18.

ORIENTAL BEEFSTEAK STRIPS

2 lb. beef round steak, cut 1 in. thick
2 tbsp. cooking oil
1/3 c. soy sauce
2 tsp. sugar
1/4 tsp. pepper
1 clove of garlic, minced
3 carrots
2 green peppers, cut in 1-in. squares
8 green onions, cut in 1 1/2-in. pieces
1/2 lb. mushrooms, halved
1 8-oz. can water chestnuts, halved
2 tbsp. cornstarch

Cut round steak into strips 1/8 inch thick and 3 to 4 inches long. Brown strips in oil. Pour off drippings; measure. Add enough water to make 1 cup. Combine with soy sauce, sugar, pepper and garlic; add to meat. Cover; cook slowly for 45 minutes. Cut carrots lengthwise into thin strips; cut strips in half. Add carrots, green peppers, onions, mushrooms and water chestnuts to meat; cover. Continue cooking 15 minutes. Combine cornstarch and 1/4 cup water. Add to cooking liquid to thicken for gravy. Serve with cooked rice. Yield: 6-8 servings.

EMPRESS OF THE EAST SALAD

3/4 head Chinese cabbage, torn
1/4 lb. spinach, torn
1/2 bunch curly endive, chopped
1 c. cubed Swiss cheese
Milk
1 tbsp. toasted sesame seed
2 med. white turnips, pared and cut
   in julienne strips
Cherry tomatoes
Ginger dressing

Toss together chilled greens in a large bowl. Dip cheese in milk, then in sesame seed to coat. Arrange cheese, turnips and cherry tomatoes on greens. Serve with Ginger Dressing. Yield: 8 servings.

Ginger Dressing

2 tbsp. all-purpose flour
2 tbsp. (firmly packed) light brown sugar
1 tsp. salt
1 tsp. ground ginger

Dash of cayenne pepper
1 c. milk
1 egg, beaten
1/4 c. white wine vinegar
1 tsp. butter
1 c. sour cream

Combine flour, sugar, salt, ginger and cayenne in saucepan. Add milk to egg; gradually stir into flour mixture. Cook over medium heat, stirring constantly, until thick. Cook 1 additional minute. Gradually stir in vinegar then butter. Cool. Fold in sour cream. Yield: 2 cups.

ALMOND BAVARIAN

1 env. unflavored gelatin
1/2 c. sugar
1/8 tsp. salt
2 egg yolks, slightly beaten
1 1/4 c. milk
1/2 tsp. almond extract
2 egg whites
1 c. whipping cream, whipped
Apricot Sauce
Toasted slivered almonds

Combine gelatin, 1/4 cup sugar and salt in a saucepan. Mix together egg yolks and milk. Add to gelatin mixture. Heat over low heat until gelatin is dissolved. Stir in almond extract. Chill until mixture mounds slightly. Beat egg whites to soft peaks. Beat in 1/4 cup sugar gradually until stiff peaks form. Fold into gelatin mixture. Fold in whipped cream. Turn into eight 5-ounce molds. Chill until set. Serve topped with Apricot Sauce and toasted slivered almonds. Yield: 8 servings.

Apricot Sauce

1 1/2 c. apricot nectar
1/2 c. sugar
1 tsp. fresh lemon juice
1/2 c. dried apricot halves, quartered

Combine apricot nectar, sugar and lemon juice in saucepan. Add apricots; cover. Simmer 20 to 25 minutes or until apricots are tender. Chill. Yield: 1 1/2 cups.

Photograph for these recipes on page 35.

DRUMMER'S DUMPLINGS AND ROUND STEAK

1 2-lb. round steak, cubed
1 chopped onion
1 bay leaf
1 can cream of chicken soup
1 can onion soup
1 can cream of celery soup
1 tbsp. Worcestershire sauce
1 4-oz. can mushrooms, drained
1 1/3 c. flour
1 No. 3 can green peas, drained
1 egg
1/3 c. milk
2 tbsp. oil
1 1/2 tsp. baking powder
1/2 tsp. salt
Dash of sage (opt.)
2 tbsp. minced fresh parsley

Place steak cubes in a 9 x 9-inch casserole. Combine onion, bay leaf, soups, Worcestershire sauce, mushrooms and 1/3 cup flour. Pour the soup mixture over steak cubes; cover. Bake in a preheated 350-degree oven for 2 hours. Stir well; add peas. Beat egg, milk and oil together until blended. Sift remaining 1 cup flour, baking powder, salt and sage together. Stir into egg mixture until moistened. Fold in parsley. Drop batter by spoonfuls over casserole; cover. Bake at 400 degrees for 25 minutes longer or until dumplings are done.

LEMON VEAL SUPREME

3 eggs
1/2 c. lemon juice
6 thinly sliced veal cutlets
Bread crumbs
Cooking oil
1 lb. Gruyere cheese
2 pt. heavy cream

Beat eggs and lemon juice together. Dip veal into egg mixture; dip into crumbs. Refrigerate for 1 hour. Fry veal in small amount oil, browning on both sides. Place in shallow baking dish. Arrange cheese slices over veal; add cream. Bake at 350 degrees until cheese melts and cream bubbles. Yield: 6 servings.

DOUBLE TIME VEAL CUTLETS

2 lb. veal round steak, 1/2 in. thick
1/4 c. flour
1 tsp. salt
1/2 tsp. pepper
3/4 tsp. monosodium glutamate
1 egg, slightly beaten
1 tbsp. milk
1 c. fine dry bread crumbs
5 tbsp. butter

Wipe veal with damp cloth. Pound meat with back of knife. Cut into four servings. Combine flour with seasonings; coat veal with flour mixture. Combine egg and milk. Dip veal into egg mixture. Coat with bread crumbs. Heat butter in skillet for 3 minutes. Add veal. Cook over medium heat for 20 minutes on each side. Yield: 4 servings.

VEAL SCALLOPINI

1 1 1/2-lb. veal steak, 1/2 in. thick
1 tsp. salt
1 tsp. paprika
1/2 c. salad oil
1/4 c. lemon juice
1 clove of garlic, split
1 tsp. mustard
1/4 tsp. nutmeg
1/2 tsp. sugar
1/4 c. flour
1 med. onion, thinly sliced
1 green pepper, cut in strips
1 can chicken bouillon
1/4 lb. mushrooms, sliced
1 tbsp. butter
6 pimento-stuffed olives, sliced

Cut veal into serving pieces. Combine next 8 ingredients; mix well. Place veal in 1 layer in baking pan. Pour sauce over veal, turning veal to coat well. Let stand for 15 minutes. Remove garlic. Drain veal; reserve sauce. Dip veal into flour. Brown in a small amount of hot fat in skillet. Add onion and green pepper. Combine chicken bouillon with reserved sauce; pour over veal. Simmer, covered, for 40 minutes or until tender. Brown mushrooms in butter in small skillet. Add mushrooms and olives to veal mixture. Stir well. Simmer for 5 minutes longer.

Top each cutlet with 1 tomato and 1 avocado wedge. Top with 3 tablespoons Sauce Mornay. Brown slightly under broiler. Serve with green noodles and tossed salad, if desired.

Sauce Mornay

3 tbsp. margarine
3 tbsp. flour
1 c. light cream or milk, heated
1/2 c. grated Parmesan cheese
Salt and pepper to taste
Nutmeg to taste
Hot sauce to taste

Combine margarine and flour in skillet. Simmer, stirring, over low heat for 2 to 3 minutes. Pour in cream gradually; stir until thickened. Add cheese; blend until smooth and cheese is melted. Season with salt, pepper, nutmeg and hot sauce. Yield: 6 servings.

VEAL PARMIGIANA

3 veal steaks
1 c. bread crumbs
1/2 c. grated Parmesan cheese
Salt and pepper to taste
Garlic powder to taste
2 eggs
2 tbsp. milk
Olive oil
1 med. onion, chopped
1 lg. can whole tomatoes
1   12-oz. can tomato paste
1 tsp. oregano
1 tsp. sweet basil
6 slices mozzarella cheese

Halve steaks. Combine next 4 ingredients. Beat eggs lightly with milk. Dip veal into egg mixture. Coat with crumb mixture. Fry in oil in skillet until golden brown on both sides. Place in baking dish. Saute onion in pan drippings. Add tomatoes, tomato paste, 3/4 cup water, oregano, basil, salt, pepper and garlic powder; blend thoroughly. Simmer, covered, for 30 minutes. Pour sauce over steaks. Bake, covered, at 350 degrees for 45 minutes. Place mozzarella cheese on steak. Bake until cheese is melted. Serve with spaghetti.

VEAL RAGOUT MANCINI

1 lb. stewing veal, diced
2 oz. cooking oil
2 slices onion
2 slices red or green pepper (opt.)
1 can tomato soup
1 tbsp. paprika
1 c. water
1/4 tsp. salt
Dash of pepper
1/2 c. mushrooms, sliced

Lightly brown veal in cooking oil. Add onion and red pepper; cook until vegetables are soft. Add soup, paprika, water, salt and pepper; cover. Simmer for 1 hour. Add mushrooms last 15 minutes of cooking time. Yield: 6 servings.

VEAL CUTLET MONTMORENCY

Melted margarine
Olive oil
6   5-oz. breaded veal cutlets
1 lg. peeled tomato
1 lg. peeled avocado
Sauce Mornay

Combine small amounts of margarine and olive oil in skillet. Saute cutlets until golden. Place in shallow baking dish. Cut tomato and avocado into 6 wedges.

Pork Parade

The meat with the fanfare of flavors, that's pork, the maestro of variety. Many a family starts and ends the day's mealtimes with pork, as they awake to the aroma of crispy-fried bacon for breakfast, look forward to hearty pork chops for supper, and relax with a zesty ham sandwich for lunch. Thrifty, industrious Germans favor pork in their satisfying cuisine. Frugal pioneer cooks depended upon its nutritious variety, because it was so easy to cure and preserve with very little waste. A day or two each fall was set aside just for preparing a storehouse of appetizing pork products — smoked hams, spicy sausages, salt pork for cooking, as well as ribs, roasts, chops, and even pickled delicacies such as knuckles, feet, and snouts! The same cuts are as popular today as they ever were, and are available daily in supermarket meat sections, delicatessens, and neighborhood grocery stores. Traditionally, people have felt that pork needed to be cooked a high temperature until well done to avoid the danger of trichnosis. Modern day pork is usually fed on sterile food alone. The chances of trichnosis being present in commercial brands of pork, has practically been eliminated. As a result, today's pork dishes can be as easily prepared and just as flavorful as any other meat. Now that has to be music to all pork lover's ears!

If you think of pork chops as just "dull old pork chops," try an upbeat version such as *Tuneful Tenderloin Cutlets.* And ham? It will take the spotlight for sure when presented as *High-Pitched Ham Salad.* Sausage shines as *Sensational Sausage Biscuits,* while *Bacon Barcarolle* brings down the house everytime.

High school choral groups and band members believe that there's not a homemaker anywhere who can do without a dependable potpourri of recipes for pork. As the troubadour of the table, it is economical enough to be a good cook's mealtime masterpiece as often as the family calls for it.

RETAIL PORK CUTS AND HOW TO COOK THEM

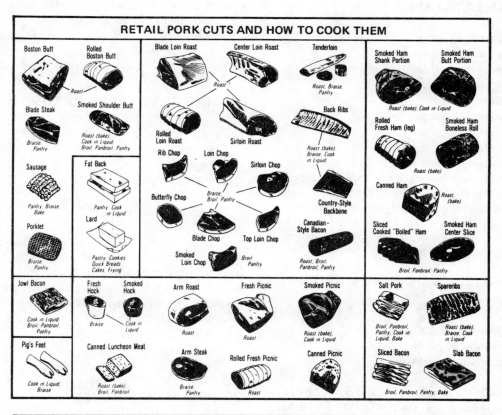

TIMETABLE FOR COOKING PORK

CUT	ROASTED AT 300 - 350 F. OVEN TEMPERATURE		BROILED	BRAISED
	Meat Thermometer Reading Degrees F.	Time Minutes Per lb.	Total Time Minutes	Total Time Hours
FRESH				
Loin				
Center	185	35 to 40		
Ends	185	45 to 50		
Shoulder				
Rolled	185	40 to 45		
Boston Butt	185	45 to 50		
Leg or Ham	185	30 to 35		
Chops				3/4 to 1
Spareribs				1 1/2
SMOKED				
Ham				
Whole	160	18 to 20		
Half	160	22 to 25		
Shank portion	160	35 to 40		
Butt portion	160	35 to 40		
Ham Slice				
(1/2 inch)			10 to 12	
(1 inch)			16 to 20	
Picnic	170	35		
Shoulder Butt	170	35		
Bacon			4 to 5	

APPLE SKILLET SUPPER

1 lb. bulk pork sausage
1 tsp. dried leaf thyme
1/3 c. (firmly packed) brown sugar
1/4 c. cider vinegar
4 c. shredded cabbage
2 red or golden Delicious apples,
cored and sliced

Break up sausage in large skillet. Add thyme; cook until browned. Add brown sugar and vinegar; mix well. Add cabbage; cook, covered, for 2 to 3 minutes or just until cabbage is wilted. Stir in apple slices. Cook 2 minutes longer. Yield: 4 servings.

APPLE CORN MUFFINS

1   12-oz. box corn muffin mix
2/3 c. milk
1 egg
2 red or golden Delicious apples, pared
and shredded or finely chopped
2 tbsp. (firmly packed) brown sugar

Combine muffin mix, milk and egg in bowl. Mix just until dry ingredients are moistened. Stir in apples. Spoon batter into 12 greased muffin cups. Sprinkle with brown sugar. Bake in 425-degree oven for 15 to 20 minutes or until golden brown. Yield: 12 muffins.

Photograph for these recipes on page 36.

MUSICAL MUSHROOMS WITH SAUSAGE

Fresh mushrooms
Tabasco sauce
Worcestershire sauce
Hot sausage
Sharp Cheddar cheese, grated
Bacon bits

Wash mushrooms and remove stems. Place mushrooms in flat baking dish. Place 1 drop of Tabasco sauce and 2 drops of Worcestershire sauce in each mushroom. Stuff each with sausage. Sprinkle with Cheddar cheese. Top each with bacon bits. Broil until brown. Be careful not to overcook. Mushroom stems may be sauteed in a mixture of butter, Tabasco sauce,

Worcestershire sauce and lemon juice. These may be used as an accompaniment to any meat dishes.

Bill Sloan
Huntsville High School
Huntsville, Alabama

PIGS IN THE BLANKET OF SONG

2 c. flour
3 tsp. baking powder
1/2 tsp. salt
2 tbsp. shortening
Milk
1 lb. ground pork sausage

Mix flour, baking powder, salt and shortening in bowl; add enough milk to make soft dough. Divide in two parts; roll out on floured board, about 1/4 inch thick. Cut into 6 squares. Place rolls of pork sausage in square; roll with dough. Pinch ends together. Place on cookie sheet. Bake at 350 degrees for 30 minutes; serve hot. Yield: 6 servings.

SAUSAGE-NUT PATTIES IN ORANGE CURRY SAUCE

10 lb. mild pork sausage
5 c. quick-cooking oats
Curry powder
1 qt. chopped peanuts
1 c. sugar
1/2 c. cornstarch
2 tsp. salt
3 tbsp. nutmeg
1 gal. orange juice

Combine sausage, oats, 2 teaspoons curry powder and peanuts; shape into small patties. Brown the patties evenly on both sides in a large skillet; drain well on absorbent paper. Place patties in baking pans. Combine sugar, cornstarch, salt, nutmeg, 1 tablespoon curry powder and orange juice, stirring until blended. Pour orange sauce over patties. Bake in a preheated 350-degree oven for 1 hour and 30 minutes, basting twice during baking time. Patties may be prepared and refrigerated until baking time.

Recipes for this photograph on page 29.

SENSATIONAL SAUSAGE BISCUITS

    2 c. sifted all-purpose flour
    3 tsp. baking powder
    1 tsp. salt
    4 tbsp. shortening
    2/3 c. milk
    1 pkg. cooked link sausage

Sift dry ingredients together. Cut in shortening until mixture is consistency of cornmeal. Add milk, stirring with fork, to make a soft dough. Roll dough about 1/4 inch thick. Cut into rounds. Wrap around sausage links. Bake at 400 degrees for 10 to 15 minutes. Serve hot. Yield: 16 servings.

HOT SAUSAGE AND APPLE SANDWICH

    1 lb. sausage
    3 apples, sliced
    Buttered toast

Shape sausage into round patties, 1/2 inch thick. Fry until browned and tender. Remove from pan; keep sausage hot. Saute apple slices in small amount of sausage drippings. Place sausage patty and apple slice on each piece of buttered toast. Garnish with bacon curls. Yield: 4 servings.

CANADIAN BACON WITH ORANGE SAUCE

    12 1/4-in. thick slices Canadian
       bacon
    6 thin onion slices
    6 orange slices, peeled
    2 tsp. sugar
    1 tbsp. cornstarch
    1 c. orange juice

Recipes for this photograph on page 34.

    1 orange, peeled and sectioned
    2 tsp. grated lemon rind

Preheat oven to 300 degrees. Arrange 6 slices Canadian bacon in greased, shallow 1 1/2-quart baking dish. Top each with onion slice, orange slice and another bacon slice. Bake for 30 minutes. Mix sugar and cornstarch together in saucepan; blend in orange juice, mixing well. Cook, stirring constantly, until thickened and clear. Stir in orange sections and lemon rind; heat thoroughly. Serve orange sauce over Canadian bacon. Yield: 6 servings.

CANADIAN BACON-BROWN SUGAR TREAT

    2 lb. unsliced Canadian bacon
    5/8 c. (firmly packed) brown sugar
    1/2 tsp. dry mustard
    Unsweetened pineapple juice
    Pineapple slices
    1 tbsp. butter

Place bacon on baking sheet. Combine 1/2 cup brown sugar, mustard and 1/2 cup pineapple juice. Spread over bacon. Bake at 325 degrees for 1 hour, basting at 15-minute intervals with drippings. Simmer pineapple slices in butter, remaining brown sugar and 1 tablespoon pineapple juice until brown. Place bacon on serving platter. Garnish with pineapple slices. Yield: 8 servings.

BACON BARCAROLLE

    2 1/2 c. coarse bread crumbs
    1 egg
    Salt and pepper to taste
    1 celery stalk, chopped
    Chopped onion (opt.)
    15 slices bacon

Combine all ingredients except bacon. Place 1 heaping teaspoon mixture on 1 end of each bacon slice. Roll bacon around dressing; secure with toothpick or small skewer. Broil, turning frequently to brown on all sides; baste with drippings. Yield: 4-5 servings.

SPICY PINEAPPLE GLAZE FOR HAM

1 whole ham
1   13-oz. can crushed pineapple
1   12-oz. can apricot-pineapple nectar
1/4 c. catsup
1 tsp. dry mustard
1 tbsp. Worcestershire sauce

Prepare ham as desired for baking. Combine pineapple, nectar, catsup, mustard and Worcestershire sauce in saucepan. Heat to simmering. During last 30 to 40 minutes of baking, spread glaze over ham. Baste occasionally. Yield: 3 cups glaze.

Photograph for this recipe on page 32.

HAM AND PORK LOAF POLKA

2 lb. fresh pork
1 lb. smoked ham
2 eggs, slightly beaten
1 c. milk
3 c. corn flakes
1 tsp. salt
Pepper to taste
1/4 tsp. dry mustard

Grind pork and ham together. Combine all ingredients in a large bowl; shape into loaf. Place the loaf in a baking pan; cover. Bake in a preheated 350-degree oven for 2 hours. Reduce oven temperature to 300 degrees. Bake, uncovered, for 15 minutes longer.

HAM IN MUSHROOM-CHEESE SAUCE

2 tbsp. chopped onion
1 tbsp. butter or margarine
1 can cream of mushroom soup
1 c. shredded sharp cheese
1 tbsp. sherry (opt.)
1 c. diced cooked ham
2 tbsp. chopped pimento
1 tbsp. parsley
Patty shells

Saute onion in butter in saucepan until browned and tender. Blend in soup, cheese and sherry; cook over low heat until cheese is melted, stirring frequently. Add ham, pimento and parsley; heat thoroughly. Serve in patty shells. Peas may be added, if desired. Turkey or chicken may be substituted for ham.

HIGH PITCHED HAM SALAD

3 c. diced cooked ham
1 c. diced celery
1/2 c. chopped stuffed olives
2 hard-boiled eggs, diced
2 tsp. minced onion
1 tbsp. lemon juice
2 tsp. prepared mustard
Dash of pepper
3/4 c. mayonnaise or salad dressing
1 c. crushed potato chips

Combine all ingredients except potato chips; mix well. Place in 8 x 2-inch round baking dish. Sprinkle with potato chips. Bake at 400 degrees 20 to 25 minutes. Yield: 6-8 servings.

SAUCY HAM CONCERTO

1 pkg. long grain rice and wild rice
1 pkg. frozen chopped broccoli
1 c. mayonnaise
1 can cream of celery soup
1 tsp. curry powder
1 sm. canned ham, cubed
Parmesan cheese (opt.)

Cook rice and broccoli according to package directions. Combine mayonnaise, soup and curry powder. Place rice in buttered casserole; arrange drained broccoli over rice. Place ham cubes over broccoli; pour soup mixture over ham. Top with Parmesan cheese. Bake, covered, in 350-degree oven for 45 minutes or until bubbly. Yield: 6 servings.

BOILED SUGAR-CURED HAM

1   20-lb. (or more) sugar-cured ham
1 whole apple
1 c. vinegar
1 c. (firmly packed) brown sugar
1 sm. bag mixed spices

3 bay leaves
Whole cloves

Trim and clean ham; soak in cold water for 24 hours. Remove from water; place in large container with cover. Cover with water; add remaining ingredients except cloves. Bring to a boil. Reduce heat and cook slowly for 20 minutes per pound. Test for doneness with fork. Remove from heat. Let stand in closed container until cold. Remove from container; skin and wipe dry. May serve immediately or spread additional brown sugar over fat side; score and push cloves into fat. Bake in 400-degree oven until brown.

OLD VIRGINIA HAM WITH RED-EYE GRAVY

1 lg. center-cut ham slice, 1/2 in. thick
1/8 tsp. salt
1/2 c. strong coffee

Slash fat on edge of ham in several places. Place ham in hot skillet; brown quickly on one side. Turn; brown lightly on other side. Simmer for 15 minutes or until tender. Remove from pan; place on heated platter. Sprinkle salt in hot skillet; add coffee. Boil for 2 minutes. Pour over ham. Serve with biscuits.

HALF NOTE HAM PARMESAN

1 lb. cooked ham
1 8-oz. package spaghetti
3/4 c. grated Parmesan cheese
2 tbsp. chopped onion
1/3 c. butter or margarine
1/4 c. flour
2 c. light cream
1 4-oz. can mushrooms
3/4 c. dry white wine (opt.)
1/3 c. sliced green olives
1 pimento, chopped
Oregano to taste
Pepper to taste

Cut ham in julienne strips. Cook spaghetti according to package directions; drain. Toss spaghetti with 1/2 cup cheese. Spread in large greased casserole; keep warm. Saute onion in butter in skillet. Remove onion; reserve. Blend flour into butter remaining in skillet; stir in cream gradually. Cook, stirring, until thickened. Blend in mushrooms, wine, reserved onion, ham, olives, pimento and seasonings. Spoon over spaghetti. Sprinkle with remaining cheese. Broil 4 to 6 inches from heat until golden. Yield: 8 servings.

HAM PATTIES WITH SOUR CREAM

2 c. ground cooked ham
1/2 c. soft bread crumbs
1/4 c. chopped green onion
1/3 c. milk
1 slightly beaten egg
Dash of pepper
1 c. sour cream

Combine all ingredients except sour cream. Shape mixture in 6 small or 4 large patties. Brown slowly on both sides in a small amount of hot fat. Heat sour cream until hot. Serve with patties.

HAM-ASPARAGUS ROLLS

24 lg. asparagus spears, cooked
6 slices boiled or baked ham
Salt and pepper to taste
Melted butter
1/3 c. flour
2 tsp. minced onion
2 c. milk
1/2 c. grated American cheese
1/4 c. sliced ripe olives

Arrange 4 asparagus spears on each slice ham. Sprinkle with salt and pepper; brush with melted butter. Roll ham over to enclose asparagus; arrange in shallow casserole. Combine 1/4 cup butter, flour and 1 teaspoon salt; add onion and milk. Cook, stirring, until thick. Add cheese and olives; pour over casserole. Bake in 350-degree oven for 25 minutes.

HAM AND MACARONI SCALLOP

1   8-oz. package macaroni
2 tbsp. butter
1 tbsp. flour
1 c. milk
1/4 tsp. pepper
1 c. minced ham
1/3 c. grated cheese
1/2 c. buttered crumbs

Break macaroni into short lengths; cook in boiling salted water for 9 minutes. Blend butter and flour until smooth. Add milk; stir until mixture boils. Season with pepper. Arrange layers of macaroni, cheese, ham and sauce in buttered casserole. Top with mixture of buttered crumbs and additional grated cheese. Bake 20 to 30 minutes in 375-degree oven. Yield: 6 servings.

FRESH HAM WITH CRANBERRY STUFFING

2 c. fresh cranberries, chopped
6 sprigs of parsley, chopped
6 slices day-old bread, crumbled
1 stalk celery, chopped
Juice of 1/2 orange
2 tbsp. sugar
1 tsp. salt
1/2 tsp. marjoram
1   10 to 12-lb. fresh ham, deboned

Preheat oven to 500 degrees. Combine all ingredients except ham; mix stuffing well. Fill ham cavity loosely with stuffing; sew edges together. Cut off rind; score fat. Bake for 30 minutes. Reduce oven temperature to 300 degrees. Bake for 3 hours and 30 minutes or until tender. Yield: 12 servings.

BARBECUED PORK IN A HURRY

1 med. onion, diced
1/2 c. diced celery
2 tbsp. brown sugar
1 1/2 tsp. dry mustard
3 tbsp. vinegar
1 c. catsup
1/4 c. lemon juice
3 tbsp. Worcestershire sauce
1 c. chicken broth
2 to 3 lb. cooked pork

Combine all ingredients except pork in saucepan; cook for 10 minutes. Shred pork; place in cooked sauce. Heat through. May serve on sandwich buns with coleslaw, if desired.

POPULAR PORK TENDERLOIN

1 med. onion, diced fine
2 carrots, diced fine
4 tbsp. bacon fat
2 whole pork tenderloins
1/4 c. flour
3/4 tsp. salt
1/4 tsp. paprika
Chili peppers to taste
1 bay leaf
1/2 c. boiling water
1/2 c. sour cream

Saute onion and carrots gently in fat in heavy frypan or Dutch oven until golden. Remove from pan. Roll pork in flour; brown over medium heat in frypan. Add onion, carrots, salt, paprika, peppers, bay leaf and boiling water. Simmer, covered, for about 45 minutes or until pork is tender. Add sour cream; stir well. Simmer for 15 to 20 minutes longer. Do not overcook or pork becomes stringy. Cut in 3/4-inch slices; serve with sauce. Yield: 5-6 servings.

TUNEFUL TENDERLOIN CUTLETS

1 pork tenderloin
1 beaten egg
Bread crumbs
Cooking oil
Tomato sauce
2 tbsp. butter
2 tbsp. flour
1 c. chicken stock
Salt and pepper to taste
1/8 tsp. nutmeg
1 c. half and half
1 1/2 c. grated Cheddar cheese

Cut pork into 1-inch slices; pound to flatten. Dip each pork slice into egg; roll in bread crumbs. Brown in hot oil in a large skillet. Add a small amount of water. Simmer, covered, for 30 minutes. Coat a baking dish with tomato sauce. Arrange pork slices in baking dish. Melt butter in a double boiler; stir in flour until bubbly. Add stock, gradually, stirring constantly. Season with salt, pepper and nutmeg. Add half and half gradually, stirring until smooth and thickened. Stir in 1 cup cheese; heat until cheese is melted. Pour sauce over the pork slices. Top with remaining cheese. Place under broiler until cheese topping melts and bubbles.

PORK TENDERLOINS AND SWEET POTATOES

4 to 6 pork tenderloins
Salt and pepper to taste
1/4 tsp. powdered sage
6 peeled sweet potatoes

Brown pork tenderloins quickly in drippings in 450-degree oven. Sprinkle with salt, pepper and powdered sage. Bake 45 minutes; baste every 15 minutes. Parboil sweet potatoes for 10 minutes; drain. Place in pan with meat. Bake until soft, basting frequently. Yield: 4-6 servings.

HERB-STUFFED PORK CHOPS WITH WINE SAUCE

6 double pork chops, with pockets
Salt and freshly ground pepper
  to taste
1/4 c. butter
3/4 c. chopped onion
1/4 c. chopped celery
2 c. bread crumbs or cubes
1 tsp. crushed fennel seed
1/2 c. minced parsley
1/4 c. half and half
Dry white wine
Cornstarch

Sprinkle pork chops inside and out with salt and pepper. Melt 3 tablespoons butter in heavy skillet. Add onion and celery; saute until onion is transparent. Stir in bread crumbs, fennel seed and parsley; remove from heat. Add enough half and half to moisten. Stuff pork chop cavities with bread crumb mixture; close openings with toothpicks. Melt remaining butter in Dutch oven. Add pork chops; saute until browned on both sides. Add wine to a depth of 1/4 inch. Bake, covered, in preheated 350-degree oven for 1 hour. Transfer pork chops to warm platter; keep hot. Bring pan juices to a boil. Mix 1 teaspoon cornstarch for each cup of pan juices with enough water to make a thin paste. Stir into pan juices; cook until thickened, stirring constantly. Serve sauce over pork chops.

BARBECUED PORK CHOPS

1/2 c. chopped onions
1/4 c. salad oil
2 tbsp. brown sugar
1 tbsp. hot sauce
1 c. chili sauce
1/2 tsp. salt
1/4 tsp. paprika
1/4 c. lemon juice
1/2 c. water
1 pkg. noodles, cooked
1 to 1 1/2 lb. pork chops, browned

Place cooked noodles in shallow baking dish. Arrange pork chops on top. Cover with barbecue sauce. Bake at 350 degrees 30 minutes. Heat onions in salad oil until brown. Add remaining ingredients except noodles and pork chops. Simmer for 15 minutes.

PEDAL PORK TENDERLOIN

1 3-lb. pork tenderloin
Soy sauce
Garlic salt to taste
1/4 c. tart orange marmalade
1/4 c. dry sherry
1 can apricot halves, drained

Place pork in a foil-lined baking pan. Rub pork well with soy sauce; sprinkle with garlic salt. Bake in a preheated 350-degree oven for 1 hour. Combine marmalade and sherry in a saucepan; heat until blended. Spread marmalade mixture over pork. Bake for 30 minutes longer, basting frequently. Increase oven temperature to 375 degrees for about 5 minutes to glaze pork. Drain pan drippings from pork into a saucepan. Add apricots; heat through. Serve with pork. May serve with rice, if desired.

APRICOT-GLAZED PORK CHOPS

1 1-lb. 14-oz. can whole apricots
1 tbsp. bottled steak sauce
1 tsp. salt
6 pork chops, cut 1/2 in. thick
1 tsp. whole cloves

Drain syrup from apricots into medium-sized pan. Stir in steak sauce and salt. Bring to a boil; reduce heat. Simmer until syrup thickens slightly, about 20 minutes. Brush chops on both sides with half the syrup. Arrange in a single layer in 13 x 9 x 2-inch baking dish. Bake, uncovered, in 400-degree oven for 30 minutes. Turn chops; skim off excess fat. Stud apricots with cloves. Arrange around chops. Brush with remaining syrup. Reduce temperature to 350 degrees. Bake 30 minutes longer or until chops are tender, brushing with glaze. Yield: 6 servings.

PORK CHOPS WITH DRESSING

6 loin pork chops
3 c. cubed bread
Salt and pepper to taste
Sage or poultry seasoning to taste
1/4 c. onion flakes (opt.)
Milk
Paprika

Sesame seed
Butter

Wash chops. Arrange in flat baking dish. Mix bread with salt, pepper, sage and onion flakes. Add enough milk to moisten. Spread over tops of chops. Add additional dry bread cubes to cover. Sprinkle with paprika and sesame seed. Dot with butter. Bake at 350 degrees about 1 hour. Yield: 6 servings.

PORK CHOPS WITH ORANGE RICE

6 pork chops
Salt and pepper
2/3 c. rice
1 tbsp. sugar
1/4 c. raisins
1 tbsp. grated orange rind
1 1/2 c. boiling water
6 orange slices
3 tsp. brown sugar

Brown pork chops well; drain off fat. Season with salt and pepper. Mix rice, 3/4 teaspoon salt, sugar, raisins and grated rind in a 3-quart casserole. Add water;

place in 350-degree oven for 10 minutes. Remove from oven; stir rice. Lay chops on top of rice. Top each chop with slice of orange and 1/2 teaspoon brown sugar. Bake at 350 degrees for 45 minutes to 1 hour or until chops are tender. Yield: 6 servings.

PORK CHOPS AND SCALLOPED POTATOES

4 to 6 pork chops
Salt and pepper to taste
Flour
6 c. thinly sliced potatoes
2 c. water
4 slices onions
1   10 1/2-oz. can cream of celery
  soup
1 c. evaporated milk or 1 can cream of
  mushroom soup

Season pork chops with salt and pepper. Coat chops with flour. Brown chops in hot fat in frypan; drain. Place potatoes in saucepan with water and 1/2 teaspoon salt; cover. Bring to a boil; cook for 5 to 8 minutes. Drain thoroughly. Place potatoes and onions in buttered 12 x 7 x 1 3/4-inch baking dish. Mix celery soup and evaporated milk. Pour over potatoes. Arrange browned pork chops on potatoes. Bake in 350-degree oven until potatoes are tender and pork chops well done, about 45 minutes. Yield: 4-6 servings.

GOURMET PORK CHOPS

6 loin pork chops
2 tbsp. flour
1 tsp. salt
Dash of pepper
1 can cream of mushroom soup
3/4 c. water
1/4 tsp. rosemary, crushed
1 can French-fried onion rings
1/2 c. sour cream

Trim excess fat from chops. Heat fat in skillet until about 2 tablespoons melted fat has collected; remove trimmings. Combine flour, salt and pepper; coat chops in flour mixture. Brown in hot fat; place in flat baking dish. Combine soup, water and rosemary; pour over chops. Sprinkle with half the onion rings; cover. Bake at 350 degrees for 50 minutes or until chops are tender. Uncover; sprinkle with remaining onion rings. Bake for 10 minutes; remove chops to platter. Blend sour cream into soup mixture in pan; heat through. Serve gravy with chops. Yield: 6 servings.

MUSHROOM PORK CHOPS

Salt and pepper to taste
8 pork chops, cut 1/2 in. thick
4 tbsp. flour
2 tbsp. oil
1 pkg. mushroom gravy mix

Sprinkle salt and pepper over each chop. Dredge chops in flour. Brown on both sides in skillet in oil. Place in baking dish. Pour excess oil from skillet over chops; add 1 cup water. Bake at 350 degrees for 1 hour. Prepare mushroom gravy mix according to package directions; pour over chops. Bake for 20 minutes longer. Yield: 4 servings.

BAKED FRUIT-PORK CHOPS

1 lb. prunes
4   1-in. thick rib pork chops
1 tsp. cinnamon
1/4 tsp. powdered cloves
2 tbsp. lemon juice
1/4 c. (packed) brown sugar
1 tbsp. salad oil
1 tsp. salt
1/4 c. hot water
4 med. sweet potatoes, halved

Soak prunes in hot water to cover for 5 minutes. Trim fat from chops; slit pocket in each chop. Pit and finely chop prunes. Combine prunes, cinnamon, cloves, lemon juice, brown sugar and 2 tablespoons water in saucepan. Simmer for 3 minutes. Stuff chops with prune mixture, reserving leftover prune mixture. Pour salad oil in skillet. Add chops; brown well. Remove chops to 3-quart baking dish; sprinkle with salt. Add hot water to pan drippings; stir well to loosen browned bits. Pour over chops. Spoon reserved prune mixture around chops. Bake, covered, for 30 minutes at 350 degrees. Add potatoes. Bake, covered, for 45 minutes longer. Yield: 4 servings.

GINGER PORK ROAST

    3 lb. pork loin
    1 tsp. Kitchen Bouquet
    1 tsp. honey
    1 tsp. salt
    2 tsp. ginger
    1 lg. onion, sliced

Wipe pork loin with paper towel. Place in shallow pan, fat side up. Blend Kitchen Bouquet, honey, salt and ginger; brush on roast. Roast at 350 degrees for 2 hours. Place onion slices on top 50 minutes before roast is done. Yield: 5 servings.

DRUM ROLL PORK ROAST

    1 5 to 6-lb. rolled pork roast
    Dried parsley
    2 onions, sliced
    1 c. Chianti

Preheat oven to 400 degrees. Place roast in baking pan. Sprinkle roast with parsley; top with onion slices. Bake, uncovered, for 20 minutes. Reduce temperature to 350 degrees. Pour Chianti over roast; cover. Bake for 1 hour and 30 minutes longer or until tender.

ROAST PORK WITH ORANGES

    1 4-lb. pork loin
    1 tsp. powdered sage
    Salt and pepper to taste
    1 tbsp. red currant jelly
    Grated rind of 1 orange
    Juice of 1 orange
    1/2 c. cooking sherry
    6 oranges

Rub pork with sage, salt and pepper. Place on rack in shallow roasting pan; add 1 cup water. Bake, uncovered, in 325-degree oven for 1 hour and 15 minutes. Pour off fat, leaving pan juices. Spread jelly over pork; sprinkle with orange rind. Pour over orange juice and cooking sherry. Bake for 45 minutes. Peel oranges; section partially at tops. Place in roasting pan. Bake for 5 minutes or until oranges are warm.

Transfer pork to platter; surround with oranges. Garnish oranges with sprigs of watercress. Yield: 6 servings.

MARINATED PORK ROAST

    1/2 c. soy sauce
    1/2 c. dry sherry
    2 cloves of garlic, minced
    1 tbsp. dry mustard
    1 tsp. ground ginger
    1 tsp. dried thyme
    1 4 to 5-lb. pork loin roast, boned,
       rolled and tied
    Currant Sauce

Blend soy sauce, sherry, garlic, mustard, ginger and thyme together. Place roast in plastic bag; place bag in deep bowl. Pour soy sauce marinade over roast; seal bag securely. Let marinate for 2 to 3 hours at room temperature or overnight in refrigerator, pressing bag against roast to distribute marinade occasionally. Remove roast from marinade. Place on rack in shallow roasting pan. Bake, uncovered, in 325-degree oven for 2 hours and 30 minutes to 3 hours or until meat thermometer reads 170 degrees, basting with marinade during the last 30 minutes of baking. Serve with Currant Sauce. Yield: 4-6 servings.

Currant Sauce

    1 10-oz. jar currant jelly
    2 tbsp. sherry
    1 tbsp. soy sauce

Heat currant jelly in small saucepan until melted. Add sherry and soy sauce; simmer for 2 minutes, stirring constantly.

BARBECUED SPARERIBS

    4 lb. ribs
    1 onion, chopped
    1/2 c. chopped celery
    2 tbsp. vinegar
    2 tbsp. brown sugar
    1 c. catsup
    3 tbsp. Worcestershire sauce
    1/2 tsp. prepared mustard

1/2 c. water
1/4 tsp. salt

Brown ribs in 325-degree oven for 1 hour. Pour off grease. Combine remaining ingredients; mix well. Pour over ribs. Bake until tender. More water may be added if necessary. Yield: 4 servings.

PEACHY BARBECUED RIBS

1 No. 2 1/2 can cling peach halves
3 lb. spareribs, cut into serving pieces
2 tsp. salt
1 c. catsup
2 tbsp. Worcestershire sauce
1/4 c. minced onions
2 tbsp. flour
2 tbsp. prepared mustard
1/2 tsp. ground cloves
1/2 tsp. pepper

Drain peaches; reserve syrup. Arrange ribs, meaty side up, in shallow roasting pan. Sprinkle with 1 teaspoon salt. Blend 1 cup reserved syrup with catsup, Worcestershire sauce, onions, flour, mustard, cloves, remaining salt and pepper in saucepan. Bring to a boil. Pour over ribs. Bake in 350-degree oven for about 1 hour and 30 minutes or until fork-tender, turning once. Arrange peaches around ribs. Bake for about 5 minutes longer, basting with sauce. Yield: 4-6 servings.

HAWAIIAN SPARERIBS

5 lb. spareribs, cut into single ribs
1 c. (packed) brown sugar
3 tbsp. cornstarch
1 1/2 tbsp. mustard
1 c. vinegar
1 sm. can crushed pineapple,
   with juice
3/4 c. chili sauce
1/3 c. chopped onions
1 can freestone peach slices, drained
1/4 c. soy sauce

Place ribs in large foil-lined baking dish. Bake in preheated 350-degree oven for 30 minutes. Turn ribs; drain off excess fat. Combine remaining ingredients with 1/3 cup water in saucepan. Cook over low heat,

stirring constantly, for about 5 minutes or until thick and transparent. Spoon half the sauce over ribs. Bake for 30 minutes. Turn ribs; spoon remaining sauce over ribs. Bake for 30 minutes longer.

PRESSURE COOKER SPARERIBS

2 tbsp. fat
4 lb. spareribs, cut into serving pieces
1 sm. onion, chopped
2 tbsp. barbecue sauce
1 sm. can tomato soup
2 tbsp. water

Heat pressure cooker; add fat. Brown ribs in fat in cooker. Combine onion, sauce, soup and water; pour over ribs. Cook for 15 minutes at 15 pounds pressure. Cool; remove from cooker. Arrange in ovenproof serving dish. Bake in 400-degree oven until brown.

Lamb And Game With A Beat

Everytime a special occasion comes along, creative cooks want to mark the event with a meal to beat the band. They look for an entree with excitement, a flavor with bravura, and often find exactly what they want in Lamb and Game recipes. Lamb, the favored meat of the Greeks, is an extraordinary taste treat because it has a distinctive taste and a velvety-smooth texture. Most American cooks forget about lamb until spring, but because it is available all year long and is as versatile and satisfying as beef, there is every reason to use it anytime. The meat from large and small game animals was a staple in the American diet long before the modern meat industries were ever dreamed of. Today, the toothsome and superior meat of these animals is considered a delicacy by meat lovers and is the perfect change of pace needed in any cook's repertoire of meat recipes. When family and friends know you are planning to serve tender and delicious game, they are sure to look forward to the meal with great relish.

One of the best things a homemaker can do for her family as she plans the week's menu is to include dishes that vary in flavor appeal. A dish that will be sure to set your family's appetite to music is *First Chair Lamb Pilaf*. Then, set a new mealtime tempo with *Lamb Kabobs*. When the hunter in your family returns with a deer, show him how proud you are by featuring it in *Venison Ragout*.

If the rhythm you like to set in your kitchen is beginning to seem more like a rut, high school music group members suggest that you keynote lamb and game dishes on the table more often. Their savory flavors can make a cozy winter evening even warmer, or a lively summer supper quite unforgetable. The days have passed when the homemaker depended on wild game to feed her family the meat they needed. But, when you begin to include these recipes in your collection, the time for lamb and game may have just begun in your house!

OLD WORLD-NEW WORLD LAMB FONDUE

5 lb. boneless leg of lamb or shoulder
Dry sherry
Olive oil
Creamy Garlic Sauce
Avocado Sauce
Spanish Filbert-Hot Pepper Sauce

Cut lamb into 3/4-inch cubes. Marinate in sherry in refrigerator for several hours, turning frequently. Remove from refrigerator; let stand to room temperature. Drain off sherry; blot lamb cubes well. Fill fondue pot about 1/2 full with oil. Heat on stove to 375 degrees or until oil bubbles. Reheat oil as necessary to maintain temperature. Set fondue pot on stand over moderately high flame. Spear lamb cubes with fondue forks; cook to desired doneness. Transfer lamb to dinner forks; dip into desired sauce.

Creamy Garlic Sauce

6 cloves of garlic, peeled
1/4 tsp. salt
1/4 tsp. white pepper
1 tbsp. lemon juice
3 egg yolks
1 c. olive oil

Combine garlic, salt, pepper, lemon juice and 1 egg yolk in blender container; blend until smooth. Add remaining egg yolks, one at a time, beating until smooth and thick. Add oil, 1/2 teaspoon at a time, blending well. Sauce will be thick after 1/2 cup oil has been added. Add remaining oil in steady stream, blending only until thick and smooth.

Avocado Sauce

1 lg. ripe avocado
2 tbsp. lemon juice
1 sm. tomato
1/4 c. finely chopped green pepper
1/4 c. finely chopped onion
1/4 tsp. coriander
Salt and pepper to taste

Peel avocado; cut into quarters. Mash avocado with fork until smooth. Stir in lemon juice until blended. Peel tomato; cut into five pieces. Add tomato, green pepper, onion and seasonings to avocado mixture. Chill; serve cold. Garnish with additional avocado slice if desired.

Spanish Filbert-Hot Pepper Sauce

1/2 c. shelled filberts
1 sm. tomato
1/4 c. red wine vinegar
1 clove of garlic
1 tsp. salt
1/2 tsp. cayenne pepper
3/4 c. olive oil

Place filberts on baking sheet. Bake at 400 degrees for 8 to 10 minutes. Combine filberts, tomato, vinegar, garlic, salt and cayenne pepper in blender container. Blend to smooth paste. Add 1/2 cup olive oil, one teaspoon at a time, blending on medium speed. Sauce should be thick and creamy. Add remaining oil in steady stream. Chill. Serve cold with lamb fondue. Additional chopped filberts may be sprinkled over sauce if desired.

Photograph for this recipe on page 46.

CURRIED LAMB ALLEGRO

2 tbsp. butter
3 onions, chopped
2 tbsp. flour
1 tbsp. curry powder
2 c. stock
1 c. milk
2 hard-boiled eggs
1 c. diced cooked lamb
Salt and pepper to taste
Cayenne pepper to taste
Cooked rice

Melt butter; add onions. Brown; dust lightly with flour and curry powder. Cook, stirring, until well blended. Add stock gradually; stir in milk. Cool until thickened. Cut eggs into eighths; fold eggs and lamb into curry mixture. Add salt, pepper and cayenne pepper. Spread hot rice in ring on serving platter; pile lamb mixture in center. Serve chutney, chopped nuts, shredded coconut and raisins in small dishes with curried lamb and rice. Yield: 4 servings.

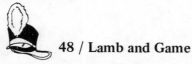

LAMB-APPLE CURRY

3 lg. apples, cored and sliced thin
1 lg. onion, sliced into rings
1 clove of garlic
Butter
2 to 3 tbsp. flour
1 tbsp. curry powder
1 tbsp. lemon juice
2 c. meat stock or bouillon
1 tsp. gravy flavoring (opt.)
Grated rind of 1/2 lemon
1/2 c. raisins
3 whole cloves
2 c. cubed cooked lamb

Saute apples, onion and garlic in small amount of butter until golden brown; remove garlic. Blend in flour and curry powder. Combine lemon juice, stock and gravy flavoring; stir into apple mixture gradually. Stir in lemon rind, raisins and cloves; cover. Simmer for 30 minutes. Add lamb; heat thoroughly. Serve with hot rice and side dish of chutney.

LAMB AND EGGPLANT ENCORE

1 lb. cubed lamb
2 tbsp. margarine
Dash of garlic salt
2 tbsp. diced onion
1 tsp. salt
Dash of pepper
6 c. cubed eggplant
4 sliced peeled tomatoes
Cracker crumbs

Saute lamb cubes in margarine, adding garlic salt, onion, salt and pepper. Stir in eggplant. Place half the mixture in 2-quart casserole; cover with half the tomatoes. Sprinkle with crumbs. Repeat. Bake at 400 degrees for 25 minutes. Yield: 4 servings.

FIRST CHAIR LAMB PILAF

2 lb. boned lamb
5 1/2 tbsp. butter
2 to 3 med. onions, sliced
1/4 tsp. cinnamon
1/4 tsp. pepper
1 1/4 tsp. salt
1 c. rice

1/2 c. raisins
3/4 c. chopped pitted prunes
3 tbsp. lemon juice
1 tbsp. minced fresh parsley
1/2 c. chopped almonds

Cut lamb into small pieces; place in heavy skillet with 4 tablespoons butter. Saute lightly. Add onions, cinnamon and pepper. Cook, covered tightly, for 2 hours and 30 minutes to 3 hours. Add 1 teaspoon salt; stir. Cool in skillet. Cook rice with remaining salt in 2 cups water; keep warm over hot water. Cover raisins with boiling water; let stand for 15 to 20 minutes. Drain. Spoon out as much liquid as possible from skillet containing lamb; reserve liquid. Skim off excess fat. Add prunes and raisins to lamb; mix well. Transfer lamb mixture to large casserole; cover with rice. Mix skimmed reserved liquid and 2 tablespoons water; spoon over rice. Cover casserole. Bake for 35 to 40 minutes at 300 degrees. Melt remaining butter; blend with lemon juice. Spoon over rice. Top with parsley. Mix rice lightly with meat to serve. Garnish with almonds. Yield: 6-8 servings.

LAMB KABOBS

1 bouillon cube
1/4 c. chopped mint
2 tbsp. wine vinegar
1 tsp. sugar
1 1/2 lb. lamb
2 tomatoes, quartered
8 sm. white onions
Salt and pepper to taste

Combine 1/2 cup water, bouillon cube and mint in saucepan. Bring to a boil. Cook for 5 minutes. Stir in vinegar and sugar. Cut lamb into 1-inch cubes. Marinate lamb in vinegar mixture for 1 hour. Drain lamb; reserve marinade. Alternate lamb cubes, tomatoes and onions on 4 long skewers. Place on rack in broiler pan. Season with salt and pepper. Broil about 3 inches from source of heat for 20 minutes. Brown on all sides. Baste frequently with remaining mint marinade. Yield: 4 servings.

LAMB CHOP MARINADE

1/2 tsp. dried marjoram
1/2 tsp. salt
1/4 tsp. pepper

Soak apricots, prunes and beans separately in water to cover for several hours. Brown chops in butter; add 1/2 cup water. Simmer for 15 minutes. Add salt, dried fruits, beans and nuts; stir well. Place chop mixture in casserole. Bake at 350 degrees for 1 hour. Remove from oven; stir in curry powder and lime. Return to oven. Bake for 30 minutes longer. Serve with rice. Yield: 4 servings.

GRILLED LAMB STEAKS

1 tsp. pepper
1 to 2 cloves of garlic, minced
3 tbsp. soy sauce
2 tbsp. catsup
1 tbsp. vinegar
4   1-in. thick lamb steaks
1   1-lb. 4 1/2-oz. can sliced pineapple
   or peaches, drained

Combine pepper, garlic, soy sauce, catsup and vinegar. Dip each lamb steak on both sides in garlic mixture. Marinate in refrigerator, turning several times for 3 hours or longer. Arrange lamb and pineapple on broiler pan. Broil 3 inches from heat for about 7 minutes on each side, brushing with marinade occasionally. Serve garnished with fruit. Yield: 4 servings.

ENGLISH LAMB CHOPS

1 tsp. salt
1/4 tsp. pepper
4 tbsp. corn oil
6 lamb chops
1 tbsp. butter
2 tbsp. flour
1 c. milk
1 tsp. Worcestershire sauce
1 c. soft bread crumbs
1/4 c. grated cheese

Combine salt, pepper and oil. Marinate chops in mixture for 30 minutes. Combine butter, flour, milk and Worcestershire sauce. Cook mixture over low heat, stirring constantly, until thickened and smooth. Broil chops 4 inches from source of heat for 5 minutes on one side. Turn chops. Spread uncooked side with white sauce. Combine crumbs and cheese; sprinkle over sauce. Place chops in baking dish. Bake at 350 degrees for 20 minutes. Garnish with parsley. Yield: 6 servings.

1/4 tsp. paprika
1 clove of garlic, minced
2 tbsp. vegetable oil
4 to 6   1-in. thick loin lamb chops

Blend first 5 ingredients together; add oil. Cover lamb chops with marinade; let stand at room temperature for 1 to 3 hours. Broil to desired doneness, basting with marinade. Yield: 2-3 servings.

ORIENTAL LAMB

1/2 c. dried apricots
1/2 c. dried prunes
2 tbsp. navy beans
6 lamb chops
1 tbsp. butter
Salt to taste
1/2 c. chopped walnuts
1 1/2 tsp. curry powder
1/2 lime, sliced

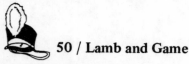

LAMB TURNOVERS

1 clove of garlic, minced
1/4 c. bacon drippings
3 tbsp. flour
1/2 tsp. salt
1 c. milk
1/2 c. minced green pepper
1 1/2 c. diced cooked lamb
1 recipe pie pastry
1 can mushroom soup
1/2 tsp. Worcestershire sauce
Pepper to taste
Leftover gravy (opt.)

Brown garlic in bacon drippings; add flour and salt, blending until smooth. Add milk. Cook over low heat until thickened. Remove from heat. Add green pepper and lamb. Cool. Cut pastry into 5-inch rounds or squares. Place 1/3 cup lamb mixture on each round. Fold over; crimp edges together well. Place on baking sheet. Bake at 425 degrees for 30 to 40 minutes. Mix remaining ingredients; heat. Serve with lamb turnovers.

LITTLE LAMB POT ROASTS

1/4 c. all-purpose flour
1 tbsp. paprika
4 lamb shanks, fat removed
1/4 c. butter
1 clove of garlic
1/4 c. currant jelly
3 tsp. salt
2 c. diced white turnips
2 pkg. frozen lima beans, thawed
1 c. half and half
1/8 tsp. pepper

Combine flour and paprika. Coat shanks on all sides with mixture. Heat butter in Dutch oven. Saute garlic until golden. Remove garlic. Place shanks in skillet; cook until browned well. Add 2 tablespoons water, jelly and 2 teaspoons salt. Simmer, covered, for 45 minutes or until shanks are just tender. Place turnips and limas on top of shanks. Cook, covered, for 30 minutes. Remove vegetables and shanks to heated platter. Stir half and half, remaining salt and pepper into pan juices. Bring to a boil. Remove from heat immediately. Pour over shanks and vegetables. Garnish with parsley. Yield: 4 servings.

CRANBERRY-LEMON GLAZED LAMB

1 4-lb. leg of lamb
Salt to taste
1 1-lb. can whole cranberry sauce
1/4 c. lemon juice
1 tbsp. grated lemon rind
3/4 tsp. rosemary

Sprinkle lamb with salt. Place on rack in roasting pan. Bake at 300 degrees for 2 hours. Combine all remaining ingredients; mix well. Spread sauce over lamb. Bake, basting occasionally, for 1 hour and 30 minutes or until meat thermometer registers 175 degrees. Yield: 6 servings.

LEG OF LAMB AND RICE NOCTURNE

1 5-lb. leg of lamb
1 clove of garlic, quartered
1 tsp. dried mint
1/2 tsp. marjoram
1 tsp. salt
1 tsp. pepper
1 sm. box rice
1 c. tart jelly
1 bottle catsup
3 tbsp. butter
2 tbsp. mint extract
Crushed fresh mint (opt.)

Cut pockets in lamb; insert garlic. Season with dried mint, marjoram, salt and pepper on fat side. Place lamb in baking pan, fat side up. Bake at 325 degrees for 1 hour and 30 minutes. Pour rice around lamb; add 2 cups boiling water. Bake for 1 hour longer, adding water if necessary to keep rice moist. Combine remaining ingredients in saucepan; heat until jelly and butter are melted and sauce bubbles. Serve lamb on platter surrounded by rice and topped with sauce. Yield: 8-10 servings.

BROILED LAMB PARISIENNE

1 7-lb. leg of lamb, boned
1/2 c. salad oil

1/4 c. lemon juice
1 tsp. salt
1/4 tsp. pepper
1 tsp. oregano
1/2 tsp. basil
2 bay leaves
2 cloves of garlic

Wipe lamb with damp paper towels. Combine remaining ingredients in jar with tightfitting lid; shake vigorously. Place lamb in large baking dish; pour marinade over lamb. Refrigerate, covered, for 12 hours or overnight, turning occasionally. Place lamb, fat side down, on broiler rack. Broil 4 inches from heat for 20 minutes or longer on each side, brushing with marinade. Yield: About 8 servings.

HERBED LEG OF LAMB

1 garlic clove
1 tsp. salt
Freshly ground black pepper
2 tbsp. olive oil
1 6-lb. leg of lamb
1 tsp. minced marjoram
1 tsp. minced thyme
1 tsp. minced rosemary
2 tbsp. flour
1 c. water

Crush garlic with salt and pepper; mix with olive oil. Spread on lamb. Sprinkle lamb with marjoram, thyme, rosemary and flour. Pour water in roasting pan with lamb. Roast at 325 degrees for 2 hours and 30 minutes, basting frequently. Yield: 6 servings.

PEASANT STEW

1 1/2 lb. lamb shoulder, cut in 1 1/2-in.
*   cubes*
1/2 c. Italian dressing
2 tbsp. shortening
1 env. dry onion soup mix
1 c. thinly sliced carrots
1/2 lb. green beans, cut up
1/2 c. sliced celery
2 tbsp. flour

Marinate lamb in Italian dressing overnight in refrigerator. Drain lamb; reserve marinade. Heat shortening in heavy saucepan. Saute lamb for 10 minutes, browning well. Drain off fat. Stir in 2 1/2 cups water, reserved marinade and onion soup mix. Simmer, covered, 45 minutes or until tender. Add vegetables. Simmer until vegetables are tender. Combine flour with 1/4 cup water. Add to broth, stirring constantly until thickened. Yield: 6 servings.

BARBECUED BEAR

1 3-lb. bear roast
Salt and pepper
1 clove of garlic, crushed
2 tbsp. brown sugar
1 tbsp. paprika
1 tsp. dry mustard
1/4 tsp. chili powder
1/8 tsp. cayenne pepper
2 tbsp. Worcestershire sauce
1/4 c. vinegar
1 c. tomato juice
1/4 c. catsup
1/2 c. water

Place roast in small roaster. Season with salt and pepper to taste; rub with garlic. Bake at 350 degrees for 1 hour or until well done. Cut into thin slices. Combine 1 teaspoon salt with remaining ingredients in heavy skillet. Simmer for 15 minutes. Add meat; simmer for 1 hour or until meat is tender.

VOCAL RABBIT STEW

1 young rabbit, cut up
1 8-oz. can tomato juice
2 garlic cloves, crushed
1 med. onion, sliced thin
1 c. oil or olive oil
1/4 c. white wine vinegar
1/4 c. green olives, sliced
1/2 tsp. hot sauce
5 or 6 potatoes, peeled and diced
1 c. sherry

Place rabbit in skillet. Add remaining ingredients except potatoes and sherry. Simmer gently for 1 hour or until tender. Add potatoes and sherry. Simmer for 30 minutes longer. Yield: 4 servings.

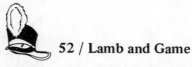

FRIED RABBIT FORTISSIMO

> 1 rabbit, dressed
> 2 tbsp. shortening

Cut rabbit into serving pieces; soak in salted water for 24 hours. Place rabbit in saucepan; fill saucepan with just enough water to cover rabbit. Bring to a boil; reduce heat. Simmer for 1 hour to 1 hour and 30 minutes or until rabbit is tender. Melt shortening in frypan; add rabbit. Fry until brown; serve immediately.

BARBECUED WILD RABBIT

> 1 c. catsup
> 1 c. barbecue sauce
> Dash of Worcestershire sauce
> Dash of prepared mustard
> 1/2 c. (firmly packed) brown sugar
> 1 med. onion, chopped
> Salt to taste
> Flour
> 1 wild rabbit, cut up
> 3 tbsp. fat

Combine catsup, barbecue sauce, Worcestershire sauce, mustard, sugar, onion and salt; set aside. Dredge rabbit pieces with flour. Brown well in fat. Place meat in 1 1/2-quart casserole. Pour sauce over meat; cover. Add water to sauce if needed. Bake 1 hour and 30 minutes at 325 degrees or until fork tender. Yield: 4-6 servings.

SQUIRREL WITH RICE

> 1   1-in. square salt pork
> 2 squirrels, cut up
> 2 qt. water
> 1 c. rice
> 1/4 c. catsup
> 1/2 onion, sliced
> Salt and pepper to taste

Dice salt pork. Saute in large saucepan until brown. Add squirrel pieces; brown lightly. Add water; simmer until tender, adding additional water if needed. Add rice, catsup, onion and seasonings. Cook over low heat, stirring frequently, until rice is tender.

MOOSE CURRY

> 1/2 peeled clove of garlic, minced
> 2 c. sliced onions
> 4 tbsp. fat
> 1 tbsp. flour
> 1 1/8 tsp. salt
> 1/8 tsp. pepper
> 1 lb. round moose steak
> 1 c. beef bouillon
> 1 tsp. curry powder
> 1/2 c. tomato juice
> 1 c. rice, boiled or steamed

Brown garlic and onions in fat. Combine flour, salt and pepper. Cut steak into 3/4-inch cubes; dredge in seasoned flour. Brown steak in fat. Add next 3 ingredients; simmer until steak is tender. Serve over rice. Garnish with chopped peanuts, chopped hard-cooked eggs or chopped green onions. Yield: 6 servings.

BAKED VENISON LOAF

> 2 lb. ground venison
> 1 lb. ground pork or ham
> 1 onion
> 1/2 lb. cracker crumbs
> 2 tbsp. salt

1 tsp. pepper
1/2 tsp. sage
2 tbsp. flour
2 tbsp. butter
1/2 c. water
1 lg. tomato, chopped or 1 can tomatoes
2 tbsp. chopped green pepper
Corn flakes

Combine first 10 ingredients. Shape into loaf. Place in 2-quart baking dish. Top with tomato, green pepper and corn flakes. Bake for 1 hour in 350-degree oven. Yield: 6-8 servings.

VENISON BURGUNDY

4 lb. venison
1/4 c. vinegar
3 tbsp. oil
3 tbsp. flour
2 tsp. salt
1 c. Burgundy
1 bay leaf

Place venison in pan; add vinegar and enough water to cover. Let stand in refrigerator for 12 hours. Drain venison; cut into cubes. Brown in hot oil. Mix flour, salt and 1 cup water; add to venison. Add Burgundy and bay leaf; cook over low heat until tender, adding water, if needed. Remove bay leaf after 1 hour of cooking. Serve over cooked rice.

VENISON RAGOUT

1 c. vinegar
Dash of Accent
Dash of salt
Freshly ground pepper
3 lb. boned venison
2 c. chopped celery
Pinch of rosemary
1/4 c. flour
1/4 c. melted butter
1/4 c. cranberry juice
1/2 pt. sour cream

Combine vinegar, 1/2 cup water, Accent, salt and pepper. Marinate venison overnight in vinegar mixture. Drain venison. Place in casserole. Add celery,

rosemary and 1 cup water; cover. Braise in oven at 350 degrees for 2 hours. Remove venison. Slice and keep warm in chafing dish. Strain stock. Combine flour and butter; stir until smooth. Add to stock. Cook, stirring constantly, until thickened. Stir in cranberry juice and sour cream. Pour over venison. Serve from chafing dish. Yield: 6 servings.

MARINATED VENISON ROAST

1 3 to 4-lb. venison roast
4 c. cold water
1/2 c. wine vinegar or wine
1 c. tomato juice
1/4 c. sugar
2 bay leaves
1/2 lemon, sliced
1 onion, sliced
2 carrots
3 stalks celery
2 cloves of garlic, chopped
1 tbsp. tenderizer
Salt and pepper to taste
1/2 c. mushrooms
1/2 c. sliced green olives
1 tbsp. parsley

Soak roast in cold salt water for 2 days before cooking. Change water several times day before serving; omit salt. Place roast in covered roasting pan. Combine remaining ingredients, except mushrooms, olives and parsley. Pour over roast; marinate overnight. Roast 2 hours and 30 minutes to 3 hours at 350 degrees. Add water if necessary; baste often. Remove meat; strain juices. Let set for a short time; skim fat from liquid. Thicken juices with flour and water paste. Add mushrooms and olives. Heat through; add parsley. Yield: 6-8 servings.

Poultry Musicale

At once delicate, appetizing, tender, and robust, poultry is probably the meat that John Philip Sousa would have marched a musical mile to enjoy. Many cooks consider chicken to be the muse of the kitchen because it is the basic ingredient in so many inspired recipes. Long gone are the days when the barnyard chicken, however special the occasion, was saved to be eaten only after it was past its egg-laying age. Today's plump, juicy chickens are plentiful, cheap, and have become a featured theme in the American cuisine. The Cornish hen, a variety obtained by cross-breeding Cornish and white Plymouth Rock fowls, is chicken's more elite, as well as more expensive cousin. This delicacy is small and succulent, and should be saved for truly elegant occasions. The turkey is America's most regal bird, and deserves all the honor and respect it receives from families on Thanksgiving Day — but, it is so good to the pocketbook that it should be a part of the regular menu throughout the year. Gone also are the days when wild fowl and game birds were so abundant that they were considered quite ordinary fare. Today, dove, quail, duck, pheasant and geese make an ordinary meal quite a sumptuous feast. Best of all, the day will never come when the chicken is not a part of American eating, because meal planning without poultry would be like rock and roll without rhythm.

Your family will demand an encore serving when you highlight *Keynote Chicken* at the dinner table. *Chicken with Shrimp Sauce* is a meal *non-plus-ultra* for the boss and his wife. A few days after Thanksgiving, *Turkey Souffle Sandwiches* are a treat with a happy tune. For a song you'll want to play again and again, *High Note Chicken Salad* never grows old!

There is no better way to keep up with the appetites of an active family and keep down the cost than to serve poultry often. High school chorus and band members are sure these Poultry recipes will bring you rave reviews every performance. A delicious and appetizing meal is an accomplishment — one you'll achieve easily and often with poultry.

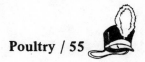

CREAMY CHICKEN SOUP

6 tbsp. butter or margarine
1/3 c. flour
3 c. chicken broth
1/2 c. milk
1/2 c. light cream
1 c. finely chopped cooked chicken
Dash of pepper

Melt butter in saucepan; blend in flour. Stir in broth, milk and cream. Cook over low heat, stirring constantly, until thickened and boiling. Add chicken and pepper; return to a boil. Serve immediately. Yield: 4 servings.

CHICKEN GUMBO

1 broiler-fryer, cut into pieces
3 tsp. salt
4 tbsp. margarine
1 med. onion, sliced
1 med. green pepper, finely chopped
2 20-oz. cans tomatoes
1 c. chicken bouillon
1 c. finely diced celery with leaves
1 bay leaf
1/4 tsp. thyme
1/2 tsp. Worcestershire sauce
1/2 tsp. Tabasco sauce
1/3 c. uncooked rice
1 can whole kernel corn
1/2 lb. okra, sliced

Sprinkle chicken with 1 teaspoon salt. Brown chicken in margarine in deep saucepan. Remove chicken. Add onion and green pepper to saucepan. Cook until tender but not brown. Return chicken to pan. Add tomatoes, bouillon, celery, remaining salt, herbs, Worcestershire sauce and Tabasco sauce. Simmer, covered, for 1 hour. Add rice, corn and okra; cook for 20 minutes longer. Serve with corn bread, if desired. Yield: 6 servings.

TOASTED CHICKEN SALAD SANDWICHES

1/4 c. chicken broth
3/4 c. mayonnaise
2 1/2 c. cooked diced chicken
1 1/2 c. diced celery
1/4 c. broken pecans
1/4 c. sliced stuffed olives
3/4 tsp. salt
Dash of pepper
Sliced bread, trimmed

Add chicken broth gradually to mayonnaise, blending well after each addition. Toss chicken with celery, pecans, olives, salt and pepper. Add mayonnaise mixture; blend lightly. Toast bread on one side; spread untoasted side with chicken salad. Top with another toasted slice. Cut in half.

CHICKEN SALAD MELODY

1 1/2 c. diced cooked chicken
1 c. diced celery
1/2 c. diced pineapple
1 c. mayonnaise
Lettuce
8 ripe olives

Toss chicken, celery and pineapple together lightly. Moisten with mayonnaise. Arrange on lettuce. Garnish with olives. Yield: 4-6 servings.

CHICKEN-CRANBERRY COMPOSITION

2 env. unflavored gelatin
1 1-lb. can whole cranberry sauce
1 c. crushed pineapple
1/2 c. broken walnuts
4 tbsp. lemon juice
1 c. mayonnaise
3/4 tsp. salt
2 c. diced cooked chicken
1/2 c. diced celery
2 tbsp. chopped parsley

Soften 1 envelope gelatin in 1/4 cup cold water. Dissolve over hot water. Add cranberry sauce, pineapple, walnuts and 1 tablespoon lemon juice. Pour into 10 x 6 x 1 1/2-inch dish. Chill until firm. Soften remaining gelatin in 1/4 cup cold water. Dissolve over hot water. Blend in mayonnaise, 1/2 cup water, remaining lemon juice and salt. Add chicken, celery and parsley. Pour over cranberry gelatin mixture. Chill until firm. Top with walnut halves. Yield: 6-8 servings.

HIGH NOTE CHICKEN SALAD

4 whole chicken breasts
1/8 tsp. ginger
1/2 tsp. nutmeg
1/4 tsp. garlic powder
Pepper to taste
1/3 c. white cooking wine
3 tbsp. lemon juice
9 hard-cooked eggs, chopped
1/2 c. chopped onion
1/4 tsp. basil
1/4 tsp. rosemary
3/4 c. slivered almonds
2 cans cream of celery soup
1 can cream of chicken soup
1 1/2 c. mayonnaise
1 1/3 c. finely crushed potato chips

Place chicken breasts in baking pan; add ginger, 1/4 teaspoon nutmeg, garlic powder, pepper, wine and lemon juice. Bake at 325 degrees until tender; let chicken cool in pan juices. Remove chicken from bones; chop. Add eggs, onion, remaining nutmeg, basil, rosemary, almonds, soups, mayonnaise and 2/3 cup potato chips. Place in baking dish. Sprinkle remaining potato chips on top. Bake at 350 degrees for 30 to 35 minutes. May be served as hot dip by heating after mixing and omitting 2/3 cup potato chip crumbs.

CHICKEN SALAD POLKA

5 chicken breasts
1 can mandarin oranges, drained
1 7-oz. jar cashew nuts
1 c. mayonnaise
1 tsp. soy sauce
1/2 tsp. curry powder
1/2 tsp. ginger
1/2 tsp. salt

Cook chicken breasts in boiling salted water until tender; cool. Remove meat from bones; cut into bite-sized pieces. Combine chicken, oranges and cashew nuts in a bowl. Blend mayonnaise, soy sauce, curry powder, ginger and salt together, blending well. Add to chicken mixture, tossing well. Chill before serving. Yield: 6-8 servings.

CHICKEN-STUFFED ARTICHOKE HEARTS

4 tsp. seasoned salt
2 tbsp. lemon juice
2 cloves of garlic, pressed
2 9-oz. packages frozen artichoke hearts
1/4 c. sour cream
1 3-oz. package cream cheese, softened
1 tbsp. minced onion
1/4 tsp. dried tarragon
1/2 tsp. soy sauce
1 6-oz. can boneless chicken

Combine salt, lemon juice, garlic, artichoke hearts and 2 cups water in a saucepan. Bring to a boil; reduce the heat. Simmer for 5 minutes. Drain artichokes; chill well. Combine sour cream, cream cheese, onion, tarragon and soy sauce, blending well. Stir in chicken. Mound a small amount of chicken mixture on each artichoke heart. Chill until serving time. Yield: 48 appetizers.

HOT CHICKEN SALAD CANTATA

2 c. cubed cooked chicken
2 c. diced celery
1 c. mayonnaise
1/2 c. chopped toasted almonds
2 tbsp. lemon juice
2 tsp. diced onion
1/2 tsp. salt
1/2 c. shredded cheese
1 c. crushed potato chips

Combine all ingredients except cheese and potato chips. Place in casserole. Top with cheese and potato chips. Bake at 450 degrees for 10 minutes. Yield: 5-6 servings.

PARTY CHICKEN DRUMETTES

1/4 c. margarine
1 c. (firmly packed) brown sugar

1 c. soy sauce
1 tsp. mustard
3 lb. chicken wing drumettes

Combine margarine, brown sugar, soy sauce, mustard and 3/4 cup water in a saucepan. Heat until margarine is melted and brown sugar is dissolved. Cool. Spread chicken wings in baking pan; pour marinade over wings. Let stand for 2 hours. Drain marinade from wings. Bake in preheated 350-degree oven for 1 hour. Reduce oven temperature to 250 degrees. Bake for 1 hour and 15 minutes longer or until tender.

CHICKEN LOAF A LA BEETHOVEN

4 c. ground or chopped cooked chicken
2/3 c. evaporated milk
1/4 c. chopped pimento
1/2 tsp. pepper
1 tsp. rosemary
1/2 tsp. marjoram
1/2 tsp. nutmeg
1 1/2 c. soft bread crumbs
2 eggs, beaten
1/3 c. chicken broth
2/3 c. diced celery
1 1/2 tsp. salt
1/2 c. milk
1 can cream of mushroom soup

Combine all ingredients except milk and soup. Turn into greased 8 1/2 x 4 1/2 x 2 1/2-inch loaf pan. Bake at 350 degrees for 45 minutes. Combine soup with milk; heat. Serve with chicken loaf.

CHICKEN FRICASSEE WITH PARSLEY DUMPLINGS

1   2 1/2 to 3-lb. fryer, disjointed
1/4 c. butter
1/2 c. diced celery
1 carrot, diced
1 med. onion, chopped
2 tbsp. minced parsley
1 bay leaf
2 tsp. salt
1/8 tsp. pepper
Parsley Dumplings
2 tbsp. flour

Wash chicken; dry. Brown in hot butter in Dutch oven. Add celery, carrot, onion, parsley, bay leaf, salt, pepper and enough hot water to cover. Simmer, covered, until chicken is tender. Drop Parsley Dumplings on top of boiling chicken mixture. Cover tightly. Cook for 15 minutes. Arrange dumplings, vegetables and chicken on large platter. Add enough water to liquid in Dutch oven to make 2 cups stock. Mix flour with 4 tablespoons water until smooth; stir into stock. Simmer until thickened; season to taste. Pour over chicken mixture. Yield: 4-6 servings.

Parsley Dumplings

1 c. sifted all-purpose flour
1/2 tsp. baking powder
1 tsp. salt
1 egg, beaten
1/3 c. milk
2 tbsp. melted fat or salad oil
2 tbsp. minced parsley

Sift flour with baking powder and salt into bowl. Add remaining ingredients; stir just until mixed.

SWEET-SOUR CHICKEN LEGS

1 tbsp. cornstarch
1 tbsp. water
1/2 c. sugar
1/2 c. soy sauce
1/4 c. vinegar
1 clove of garlic, minced
1/2 tsp. monosodium glutamate
1/2 tsp. ground ginger
1/4 tsp. ground pepper
8 to 10 chicken legs
1   1-lb. 4-oz. can pineapple chunks, drained

Combine all ingredients except chicken legs and pineapple in small saucepan. Cook and stir over medium heat until thick and bubbly. Place chicken legs in greased baking pan. Brush generously with glaze. Bake in 450-degree oven for 25 minutes, brushing with glaze twice. Turn all chicken legs; brush with glaze. Bake for 15 minutes longer, brushing twice. Arrange pineapple chunks over chicken legs. Bake for 10 minutes longer. Yield: 4 servings.

CHICKEN LIVER PATE

2 tbsp. butter
1/2 lb. chicken livers
1 3-oz. can mushrooms, drained
1 med. onion, chopped
2 tbsp. chopped chives
1/4 c. chopped parsley
1/2 c. mayonnaise
Salt and pepper to taste
Dry sherry to taste

Melt butter in skillet. Saute livers until all pink disappears. Process livers, mushrooms and onion through a meat grinder. Combine liver mixture with remaining ingredients, mixing well. Chill well before serving. Serve with crackers or melba toast rounds.

CHICKEN CACCIATORE

2 2-lb. broilers
3 tbsp. olive oil
4 cloves of garlic, minced
Salt and pepper to taste
Pinch of crumbled oregano
2 leaves basil, crumbled
1 No. 2 can solid pack tomatoes, mashed
1 4-oz. can button mushrooms
2 tbsp. butter or margarine
1/4 c. sherry
1 tbsp. minced parsley

Disjoint broilers. Heat olive oil in deep frypan. Add broiler pieces, garlic, salt, pepper, oregano and basil. Fry until browned. Add tomatoes. Saute mushrooms in butter; add to chicken. Cover; cook for 15 minutes. Remove cover; add sherry. Cook, uncovered, for 10 minutes. Sprinkle with parsley. Yield: 6 servings.

CHICKEN WITH ARTICHOKES

1 3-lb. fryer, cut up
Salt, pepper and paprika to taste
3 tbsp. butter
1 can cream of chicken soup
1/2 c. Madeira
1 1-lb. can artichoke hearts
1 sm. can mushrooms

Sprinkle chicken with salt, pepper and paprika. Brown well in butter. Transfer to ovenproof casserole. Pour soup and Madeira into drippings; stir until smooth, using slotted spoon. Add artichoke hearts and mushrooms. Pour over chicken. Bake, covered, at 350 degrees for 1 hour. Yield: 4-5 servings.

CHICKEN CADENZA

2 chickens, cut up
2 4-oz. cans mushroom caps, drained
1 can whole tomatoes, drained and
    quartered
4 bay leaves
1 c. sliced black olives
1 8-oz. bottle Wishbone Italian
    dressing
2 env. dry onion soup mix
1/2 tsp. oregano
1/2 c. dry vermouth

Arrange chickens in single layer in large pan. Place mushrooms, tomatoes, bay leaves and olives on chicken. Combine remaining ingredients. Pour over chicken. Bake, uncovered, in preheated 350-degree oven for 1 hour or until chickens are fork-tender, basting occasionally. Chickens, mushrooms, tomatoes, bay leaves and olives may be prepared ahead of time and refrigerated. Yield: 8 servings.

UKELELE CHICKEN

1 broiler-fryer, cut up
1 tsp. monosodium glutamate
2 tbsp. salad oil
1 20-oz. can pineapple chunks
2 tbsp. soy sauce
1/4 c. water
2 tbsp. cornstarch
1 c. diagonally sliced celery
2 med. tomatoes, cut into 16 wedges
1 green pepper, cut in strips

Wash and dry chicken. Sprinkle with monosodium glutamate. Let stand for 15 minutes. Brown quickly

for 1 hour or until chicken is tender. Yield: 4-6 servings.

JAPANESE-FRIED CHICKEN

4 chicken breasts
1 egg, well beaten
1 tbsp. water
1/2 c. flour
2 c. bread crumbs
Salad oil
Ginger Sauce

Bone chicken; cut into bite-sized pieces. Mix egg and water. Dip chicken in flour; dip in egg mixture. Dip in bread crumbs. Fry in hot, deep oil until browned. Dip in Ginger Sauce to serve.

Ginger Sauce

1 tsp. grated ginger
1/4 c. white wine
1/2 c. soy sauce
1/2 c. sugar
1 tsp. monosodium glutamate

Combine all ingredients; cook until sugar is dissolved.

in hot oil in skillet. Drain pineapple, reserving syrup. Add syrup and soy sauce to chicken. Simmer, covered, for 20 minutes. Combine water and cornstarch; add to chicken, stirring constantly, until thickened. Add celery, tomatoes, green pepper and pineapple. Simmer, covered, for 10 minutes longer. Serve with hot cooked rice. Yield: 4 servings.

KEYNOTE CHICKEN

1 1/3 c. flour
3 tsp. salt
1 1/2 tsp. ground sage
1/4 tsp. pepper
1 3-lb. frying chicken, cut up
1/4 c. fat
1 tsp. baking powder
3 eggs, well beaten
1 1/2 c. milk
1/4 c. butter or margarine, melted
1/4 c. chopped parsley

Combine 1/3 cup flour, 2 teaspoons salt, sage and pepper; coat chicken pieces. Brown in hot fat. Place in 2-quart casserole. Sift remaining flour, baking powder and remaining salt together. Combine eggs, milk, butter and parsley; add to flour mixture. Stir until smooth; pour over chicken. Bake at 350 degrees

PAN-FRIED CHICKEN

1 3-lb. frying chicken, cut into serving
*   pieces*
1/2 c. flour
1 1/2 tsp. salt
1/4 tsp. pepper
1 tsp. paprika
1 c. shortening

Wash chicken in cold water; drain. Mix flour, salt, pepper and paprika in paper sack. Shake chicken pieces in sack to coat thoroughly. Melt shortening in preheated 360-degree frypan. Place chicken, skin side down, in hot fat; brown on all sides. Add cold water. Reduce heat to 225 degrees. Cook for 25 to 30 minutes longer or until chicken is tender. For crisper crust, remove cover and cook at 360 degrees for an additional 5 minutes. Yield: 4 servings.

OVEN-FRIED CHICKEN WITH PARMESAN CHEESE

1 1/2 c. fine corn flake crumbs
1/4 c. grated Parmesan cheese
1/4 c. chopped parsley
2 tsp. salt
1 tsp. seasoned salt
1/4 tsp. pepper
2 3 to 3 1/2-lb. frying chickens,
cut into serving pieces
1/2 c. melted butter

Combine first 6 ingredients; mix well. Dip chicken into butter, then into cheese mixture. Arrange in two 13 x 9 x 2-inch baking dishes, allowing space between chicken pieces. Bake, uncovered, at 350 degrees for 1 hour and 30 minutes or until tender. Yield: 6-8 servings.

CREAMED CHICKEN AND BEEF OVER BAKED POTATOES

4 Idaho potatoes
3 tbsp. butter or margarine
1/4 c. finely chopped onion
2 tbsp. chopped celery
1 2 1/2-oz. jar sliced dried beef
3 tbsp. flour
2 c. milk
1/4 tsp. dried leaf thyme
1/8 tsp. pepper
1 tsp. lemon juice
1 tsp. Worcestershire sauce
1/2 c. diced cooked chicken

Scrub potatoes, dry and prick with fork. Bake in 425-degree oven for 55 to 65 minutes or until tender. Melt butter in medium saucepan. Add onion, celery and dried beef. Cook until vegetables are tender. Blend in flour. Stir in milk, thyme, pepper, lemon juice and Worcestershire sauce. Cook over medium heat, stirring constantly, until sauce comes to a boil and thickens. Stir in chicken. Remove potatoes from oven when done; cut an X in top with a fork. Push potato up with slight pressure of fingers on the side of potato. Spoon sauce over each potato. Yield: 4 servings.

Photograph for this recipe on page 69.

CASSEROLE FOR ORCHESTRA

1 can cream of mushroom soup
1 can chicken-rice soup
1 can cream of chicken soup
1 lg. can evaporated milk
1 1-lb. 14-oz. or 6 5-oz. cans boned chicken
1 can chow mein noodles
1 can sliced mushrooms
1 can water chestnuts, sliced
2 cans French-fried onion rings
1/4 c. sherry (opt.)
1/2 med. green pepper, diced
2 stalks celery, diced
Crushed potato chips

Combine all ingredients except potato chips; mix carefully. Pour into large baking pan; sprinkle crushed potato chips over top. Bake in preheated 275-degree oven for 1 hour or until heated through and bubbly.

CHICKEN CROQUETTES

2 c. cooked chicken
1 sm. onion
2 slices bread
2 eggs, slightly beaten
1/4 tsp. salt
1/2 tsp. poultry seasoning or
1/4 tsp. sage
1 c. chicken stock or creamed soup
3 tbsp. flour
Dash of pepper
1/2 c. cracker crumbs

Grind chicken, onion and bread together. Blend all ingredients except crumbs together. Shape into 6 croquettes; roll in cracker crumbs. Brown in small amount of fat in skillet. May be frozen before cooking; will keep for 4 to 6 weeks. Yield: 6 servings.

CHICKEN ENCHILADAS

1 3-lb. chicken
3 cloves of garlic, minced fine
4 tbsp. cooking oil
3 tbsp. flour

1 No. 2 1/2 can chili sauce
1 sauce can (scant) water
Pinch of oregano
Salt to taste
3 lg. onions, sliced thin
1 lb. shredded Cheddar cheese
1 can black olives
1 doz. corn tortillas

Boil chicken in water to cover until tender. Remove skin and bones; cut into small pieces. Saute garlic in 2 tablespoons oil; stir in flour. Add chili sauce, water, oregano and salt. Stir until smooth; bring to a boil. Simmer for 30 minutes. Add chicken to half the sauce. Cook onions in remaining oil until soft; add 3 tablespoons sauce to color. Place small amount of chicken mixture, onions, cheese and 2 or 3 olives on each tortilla; fold over upper half. Place in baking dish; pour in remaining sauce. Top with remaining cheese and 1 olive for each enchilada. Bake in 350-degree oven until cheese melts. Serve hot. Yield: 12 servings.

CHICKEN ALLEGRO

4 whole chicken breasts
1 pkg. corn tortillas
1 can cream of mushroom soup
1 can cream of chicken soup
1 c. milk
1   7-oz. can green chili salsa
1 grated onion
3/4 lb. grated Cheddar cheese

Wrap chicken breasts in aluminum foil; place on baking sheet. Bake in a preheated 400-degree oven for 1 hour or until done. Remove skin and bones from chicken; cut meat into bite-sized pieces. Cut tortillas into bite-sized pieces. Cover the bottom of a greased 13 x 9-inch pan with half the tortillas. Cover tortilla layer with half the chicken. Blend soups, milk, salsa and onion together. Spoon half the soup mixture over chicken. Sprinkle remaining tortillas over soup layer. Spread remaining chicken over tortillas. Spoon remaining soup mixture over chicken. Top with cheese. Chill overnight. Bake in a preheated 350-degree oven for 1 hour and 30 minutes. Yield: 12 servings.

CHICKEN SEXTET

3 chicken breasts, halved
Monosodium glutamate
Salt to taste
Pepper to taste
Paprika to taste
Butter
1 c. orange juice
2 tbsp. slivered orange rind
1 tsp. tarragon
3 c. cooked rice
1 avocado, diced
Orange and lemon slices, halved

Sprinkle chicken with monosodium glutamate, salt, pepper and paprika. Melt 1/4 cup butter in large skillet; brown chicken, turning only once. Remove from skillet. Add orange juice and rind to butter; bring to a boil. Stir to loosen brown particles from pan. Return chicken to mixture in skillet; sprinkle with tarragon. Cover; cook for about 25 minutes. Toss hot rice with 3 tablespoons butter. Add avocado. Serve chicken on rice bed; spoon sauce on chicken and rice. Garnish with orange and lemon slices. Yield: 6 servings.

CHICKEN AND CELERY AU GRATIN

2 tbsp. butter
2 tbsp. flour
1 c. chicken stock
1/4 c. light cream
Salt and pepper to taste
6 cooked chicken breasts, boned
2 c. chopped celery, parboiled
1/4 c. blanched almonds
1/2 c. grated cheese
1 c. buttered bread crumbs

Melt butter; stir in flour. Stir in chicken stock and cream gradually. Cook, stirring constantly, until thickened. Add salt and pepper. Place chicken in buttered casserole. Combine celery, almonds and cream sauce; pour over chicken. Top with cheese and bread crumbs. Bake at 350 degrees until bubbly and brown. Cooked, sliced chicken may be substituted for chicken breasts. Yield: 6 servings.

CHICKEN WITH BING CHERRIES

1/3 c. all-purpose flour
1 1/2 tsp. salt
1/4 tsp. garlic salt
1/2 tsp. paprika
3 lg. chicken breasts, cut in half
1/4 c. butter or margarine
1   1-lb. can pitted Bing cherries, drained
1 c. sauterne

Combine flour, salt, garlic salt and paprika in paper
bag. Add 2 or 3 pieces of chicken at a time to flour
mixture; shake. Heat butter in skillet. Brown chicken
in butter, turning once. Add cherries. Pour sauterne
over top. Simmer, covered, for 40 minutes or until
chicken is tender. Yield: 6 servings.

CHICKEN CHUTNEY CHORALE

6 chicken breasts
Salt and pepper to taste
1 c. flour
5 tbsp. butter
1 sm. onion, chopped
3/4 c. chutney
1/2 pt. heavy cream

Sprinkle chicken breasts with salt and pepper; dip in
flour. Saute chicken in butter in large skillet until
lightly browned; cover. Cook over low heat for 15 to
20 minutes or until done. Remove to serving platter;
keep warm. Drain all but 1 teaspoon fat from skillet.
Saute onion in fat. Add chutney; stir in cream. Heat
to boiling point. Spoon over chicken. Yield: 6
servings.

CHICKEN WITH CURRANT SAUCE

12 chicken breasts
Salt and pepper to taste
2 12-oz. jars currant jelly
12 oz. water
2 tbsp. cornstarch
2 to 4 tsp. allspice
2 tbsp. Worcestershire sauce
4 tbsp. lemon juice

Wash chicken; season. Set apart in large shallow pan.
Bring remaining ingredients to a boil; pour over

chicken. Bake, uncovered, at 350 degrees for 1 hour.
Turn chicken; bake for 30 minutes longer. Baste
occasionally; add water if sauce becomes too thick.
Yield: 12 servings.

CHICKEN WITH GRAPES
A LA SHUBERT

8 chicken breasts, halved
Flour
Butter
Salt and pepper to taste
1/2 c. chopped onions
1 clove of garlic, crushed
1 c. dry white wine
1 tsp. mace
1 c. seedless white grapes

Remove bones and skin from chicken; coat well with
flour. Melt small amount of butter in a skillet. Brown
chicken evenly; season with salt and pepper. Place
chicken in a casserole. Saute onions and garlic in pan
drippings in skillet, adding butter if necessary. Spoon
onion mixture over chicken. Pour 1/2 cup water and
wine into skillet; heat through, stirring. Pour wine
mixture over chicken; add mace and grapes. Cover.
Bake in a preheated 400-degree oven for 15 minutes.

Reduce oven temperature to 350 degrees; bake for 45 minutes longer.

CHICKEN KIEV

4 lg. chicken breasts
1/2 c. butter
2 tbsp. finely chopped parsley
2 tbsp. chopped chives
Dash of garlic powder
1/2 tsp. salt
1/2 tsp. pepper
1 tsp. Worcestershire sauce
1 egg
1/2 c. half and half
Flour
Cracker crumbs

Skin and bone chicken breasts; separate each breast into 2 fillets. Flatten between waxed paper. Cream butter; blend in parsley, chives, garlic powder, salt, pepper and Worcestershire sauce. Divide butter mixture into 8 parts on plastic wrap. Form into rolls; freeze or chill. Sprinkle breasts with additional salt. Place butter mixture part in each chicken breast; roll up. Secure with wooden picks. Beat egg and half and half. Roll breasts in flour; dip into egg mixture. Roll in cracker crumbs. Fry in deep fat for 8 to 10 minutes at 360 degrees or until golden brown. Keep warm in oven. Yield: 8 servings.

RHYTHMICAL CHICKEN SAUTE

8 lg. chicken breasts
Salt, pepper and paprika to taste
3 tbsp. each butter and olive oil
1/8 tsp. each dried tarragon and
  rosemary
3/4 lb. fresh mushrooms, sliced
Juice of 1 lemon
1 c. dry white wine
3 tbsp. sherry
3 tsp. chicken stock base
2 pkg. frozen artichoke hearts
Chopped parsley

Remove bones from chicken breasts. Cut chicken breasts in half. Season with salt, pepper and paprika.

Brown in butter and oil. Sprinkle with tarragon and rosemary. Cover; cook over medium heat for 20 to 25 minutes or until tender. Remove chicken. Add mushrooms to pan. Add lemon juice, wine, sherry and stock base. Cook for several minutes; add artichoke hearts. Cook until vegetables are tender but firm. Arrange chicken and vegetables in serving dish. Cook sauce in pan over high heat until thick. Pour over chicken mixture. Sprinkle with parsley just before serving. Yield: 8 servings.

CHICKEN WITH SHRIMP SAUCE

5 chicken breasts
Flour
1 tbsp. oil
1 green onion, chopped
1 can mushrooms, drained
1 can shrimp soup
1 sm. can shrimp, drained
1 c. milk
Sherry to taste

Roll chicken in flour; brown in hot oil in skillet. Place chicken in casserole. Saute onion and mushrooms in pan drippings. Add shrimp soup, shrimp, milk and sherry. Heat until bubbly. Pour over chicken. Bake in a preheated 375-degree oven for 45 minutes; remove cover. Bake for 10 minutes longer. Serve over cooked rice.

CANDIED CHICKEN BREASTS

Salt to taste
5 chicken breasts, halved
Flour
1 c. waffle syrup
1/2 c. white vinegar
1/2 c. catsup

Salt chicken; dip in flour. Brown on both sides in hot fat. Pour syrup, vinegar and catsup in jar; cover. Shake well. Line baking pan with aluminum foil; place chicken breasts, meaty side down, on foil. Cover with syrup mixture. Bake at 325 degrees for 1 hour and 30 minutes. Turn; baste with syrup mixture. Bake for 30 minutes longer. Yield: 10 servings.

TWO-CHEESE CHICKEN BREASTS

3 lg. chicken breasts, halved
6 1 1/2-in. squares Swiss cheese
3 tbsp. crumbled blue cheese
1/4 c. flour
1/2 tsp. salt
1/4 tsp. pepper
1 egg, slightly beaten
1/3 c. milk
1/2 c. fine dry bread crumbs
1/2 c. butter

Remove bones and skin from chicken breasts; pound chicken carefully with a mallet until thin. Place 1 slice of Swiss cheese and 1 1/2 teaspoons blue cheese on each chicken breast. Fold the short ends over cheese mixture, then fold long ends over, securing with skewers. Combine flour, salt and pepper. Coat each roll with flour mixture. Beat egg and milk together; dip rolls into egg mixture. Roll in bread crumbs to coat evenly. Let stand for about 20 minutes or until coating is set. Melt butter in a large skillet. Cook chicken rolls for about 5 to 7 minutes on each side or until golden brown. Place chicken rolls in a baking dish; pour pan drippings over rolls. Bake in a preheated 325-degree oven for 25 to 30 minutes. Remove skewers before serving.

SOUR CREAM-CHICKEN RECITAL

6 med. chicken breasts
1 3/4 c. sour cream
1/8 c. lemon juice
2 tbsp. Worcestershire sauce
2 tbsp. celery salt
1 1/2 tsp. paprika
2 tsp. salt
1/2 tsp. pepper
1 3/4 c. fine dry bread crumbs
1/4 c. melted butter or shortening

Wipe chicken breasts dry. Combine sour cream, lemon juice, Worcestershire sauce, celery salt, paprika, salt and pepper; spread over chicken breasts. Refrigerate overnight. Drain; reserve sour cream mixture. Roll chicken in bread crumbs; place in 8-inch square baking dish. Pour reserved sour cream mixture over chicken; pour butter over sour cream mixture. Bake at 350 degrees for 1 hour or until tender. Yield: 6 servings.

CORNISH HENS WITH SPICY STUFFING

3 1/2 c. stale bread crumbs
1/2 c. chopped sweet mixed pickles
1/2 c. diced dried figs
1 egg, slightly beaten
1/4 tsp. salt
1/8 tsp. poultry seasoning
1/2 c. chopped celery
1/4 c. butter
4 frozen 1-lb. cornish hens, thawed

Mix bread crumbs, pickles, figs, egg, salt and poultry seasoning together in bowl. Saute celery in butter for 1 minute. Add to bread mixture, tossing well. Stuff hens with stuffing mixture. Truss hens. Arrange on spit. Roast hens on rotisserie for 1 hour or until tender and browned. Brush occasionally with additional melted butter. Serve with additional sweet mixed pickles. Yield: 4 servings.

Photograph for this recipe on page 54.

CHICKEN AND SOUTHERN DRESSING COMBO

1 4-lb. dressed hen and giblets
Salt
4 c. corn bread crumbs
1 c. finely chopped celery
3 hard-boiled eggs, chopped
1 tsp. sage
5 biscuits, crumbled
4 tbsp. minced onion
1/2 tsp. freshly ground pepper
2 eggs, beaten
1/4 c. butter
1/4 c. flour

Cover hen and giblets with water; add 1 1/2 tablespoons salt. Bring to a boil; simmer until almost tender. Remove hen and giblets from broth; chop giblets. Place hen in baking pan. Bake at 375 degrees for 40 minutes or until well browned and tender. Bring chicken broth to a boil. Place corn bread crumbs in mixing bowl; add 3 cups chicken broth. Cover; let stand for 5 minutes. Add celery, 2 hard-boiled eggs, sage, biscuits, onion, pepper and beaten eggs; mix well. Add more broth, if needed. Pour into greased baking dish. Bake at 375 degrees for 1 hour. Melt butter. Add flour and 1/2 teaspoon salt; blend well. Add 2 cups chicken broth, giblets and remaining hard-boiled egg; cook until thick, stirring constantly. Serve with chicken and dressing.

TURKEY SOUFFLE SANDWICHES

8 slices bread, crusts removed
1/2 lb. sliced turkey
1/4 lb. sliced Swiss cheese
4 eggs
2 c. milk
2 tsp. onion salt
3/4 tsp. crushed thyme
Dash of Worcestershire sauce (opt.)

Prepare 4 sandwiches with bread, turkey and cheese. Place in greased 8-inch square baking pan. Beat eggs in bowl until frothy. Add milk, onion salt, thyme and Worcestershire sauce; blend well. Pour over sandwiches. May be refrigerated overnight. Bake in preheated 325-degree oven for 50 minutes to 1 hour or until set and golden. Serve immediately. Ham or tuna may be substituted for turkey.

TURKEY A LA KING

4 oz. medium noodles
1 can cream of chicken soup
1 c. milk
1 tsp. salt
1 1/2 c. grated American cheese
2 c. diced leftover turkey
1 c. 1/4-in. slices celery
1/4 c. diced green pepper
1/4 c. diced pimento
1 c. slivered toasted almonds
Buttered bread crumbs

Cook noodles according to package directions. Combine soup, milk and salt; cook over low heat, stirring constantly. Add cheese; stir until melted. Add turkey, celery, green pepper, pimento and 1/2 cup almonds; mix thoroughly. Place in greased casserole. Top with crumbs and remaining almonds. Bake, uncovered, at 350 degrees for about 45 minutes.

CURRIED TURKEY

1/4 lb. butter or margarine
10 tbsp. flour
5 c. turkey broth
1 tsp. salt
1/2 c. sherry
1 c. seedless raisins (opt.)
4 tsp. curry powder
1 clove of garlic, crushed
6 c. (packed) cut-up turkey
1 lg. can mushrooms
1 6-oz. package almonds, slivered

Combine butter, flour, broth and salt; cook, stirring constantly, over low heat until thick. Add sherry, raisins, curry powder, garlic, turkey and mushrooms. Brown almond slivers delicately in additional butter. Serve over turkey mixture. Serve on toast points, in patty shells, or over rice. Yield: 25 servings.

TUNEFUL TURKEY STRATA

5 slices buttered white bread
2 1/2 c. diced cooked turkey or chicken
1 c. grated Cheddar cheese
3 eggs
2 c. milk
1/2 tsp. salt
1/4 tsp. pepper
1 10 1/2-oz. can cream of chicken soup
1/2 10 1/2-oz. can cream of mushroom soup
1/2 c. water
1/2 tsp. curry powder
1 c. canned mushroom caps or pieces

Remove crusts from bread; cut into 1-inch squares. Place in 8 x 8 x 2-inch oiled casserole or glass baking dish. Add layer of turkey, then layer of cheese. Repeat layers 3 times. Beat eggs slightly. Add milk, salt and pepper; blend well. Pour over cheese layer. Cover; let stand in refrigerator overnight. Remove from refrigerator; bring to room temperature before baking. Bake in preheated 325-degree oven for 1 hour. Combine soups in saucepan; add water gradually. Add curry powder; stir until smooth. Stir in mushrooms; cook over low heat, stirring frequently, until heated through. Serve over turkey. Cooked pheasant or capon may be substituted for turkey.

Seafood Symphonies

Nature supplies us with one of the jazziest choruses of flavors to be found anywhere — in the fish and seafood we gather from our rivers, lakes, and oceans. Trout, salmon, catfish, shrimp, oysters, lobster, clams, crabs, flounder, and red snapper are all part of a much longer list of fresh and saltwater delights we can feature on our tables all the year through. In season, fresh fish is an unbeatable bargain. The same holds true for shellfish in coastal areas — in season, it's both plentiful and cheap. Fish and shellfish hold still another advantage for weight and nutrition watchers because, when compared ounce for ounce with meat and poultry, fish contains more protein and far fewer calories. Family members love it when the cook plans fish, because people associate fish with fun. A catfish fry in the South means coleslaw and hush puppies, crowds, music, and laughter. In New England, a clambake on the beach finds everyone trading sailing and fishing stories passed on to them by their grandfathers. And in the Rocky Mountains of the West, families get close to nature, camp, and grill mouth-watering trout over a campfire. Equally memorable meals can be enjoyed by any family at any time, because seafood is the basis for dozens of delicious recipes.

Keep a can of salmon handy on the shelf, then make Wednesday night special with *Super Salmon Loaf.* For dinner on a hot Sunday afternoon, *Crab Louis Mold* is a perfectly elegant and satisfying cooler. Company coming? Impress them admirably with *Baked Snapper with Crab Meat Stuffing.*

Many home economists recommend that fish should be served at least once per week, and high school choral groups and band members can't think of a better piece of advice. With all of these recipes to choose from, you'll be glad, too. Like a flourish of trumpets, the smiles on your family members' faces will assure you that delicious fish and shellfish dishes are welcome at the table anytime!

CODFISH BALLS BARCAROLLE

1 1/2 c. or 1/2 lb. shredded salt codfish
3 c. diced potatoes
2 tbsp. butter or margarine
1/4 tsp. pepper
1 egg, beaten

Soak codfish in water for several hours or overnight. Cook potatoes and codfish in boiling water until potatoes are tender; drain. Mash; add remaining ingredients. Beat thoroughly. Drop from tablespoon into shallow hot fat; fry until brown. Drain on absorbent paper.

BAKED HADDOCK IN CREOLE SAUCE

2 pkg. frozen haddock fillets
1/2 c. chopped onion
1/2 c. chopped green pepper
4 tbsp. margarine
1 can tomato soup
8 thin lemon slices

Place fish in greased baking dish. Cook onion and green pepper in margarine; add soup. Pour sauce over fish. Top with lemon slices. Bake at 400 degrees for 40 to 45 minutes. Yield: 4 servings.

FINNAN HADDIE FINALE

2 lb. finnan haddie
1 tbsp. finely chopped onion
2 tbsp. finely chopped green pepper
2 tbsp. finely chopped red pepper or pimento
2 tbsp. butter
1 tsp. salt
1/2 tsp. paprika
Dash of cayenne
4 tbsp. flour
2 c. light cream

Soak finnan haddie in cold water for 1 hour. Drain; cover with water. Simmer for 30 minutes. Drain; flake. Cook onion, green pepper and red pepper in butter for 5 minutes or until soft; do not brown. Add salt, paprika, cayenne and flour; stir until blended. Add cream gradually. Cook, stirring constantly, until thickened. Add finnan haddie. Serve over toast or in potato nests. Yield: About 6 servings.

MELT-IN-YOUR-MOUTH FRIED FISH

2 lb. whitefish, filleted
1 egg white
1 tsp. garlic salt
1 tsp. baking powder
1 c. flour
1 tbsp. oil
1 c. water

Cut fillets into 2-inch square pieces. Beat egg white; set aside. Combine garlic salt, baking powder and flour. Add oil; stir well. Add water; stir until well blended. Fold in egg white. Dust fish with additional flour; coat with batter. Fry in deep fat until golden brown. Yield: 5 servings.

SWISS-BAKED FILLETS

2 lb. frozen fish fillets, thawed
1 c. sour cream
1/2 c. slivered Swiss cheese
1/4 c. finely chopped scallions or onion
3/4 tsp. salt
1/8 tsp. pepper
1 tsp. prepared mustard

Arrange fillets in baking pan. Combine remaining ingredients in small bowl; spread over fillets. Bake at 350 degrees for about 20 minutes or until fish flakes easily when tested with fork. Place baking pan under broiler for 1 to 2 minutes to brown fish. Yield: 6 servings.

HALIBUT WITH WALNUTS AND CHEESE

1 1/2 lb. halibut steak
Juice of 1 lemon
Salt and pepper to taste
1/4 c. chopped walnuts
1/3 c. grated sharp cheese
2 tbsp. milk

Place halibut in buttered baking dish. Sprinkle with lemon juice, salt and pepper. Mix walnuts with cheese and milk. Season with salt and pepper. Sprinkle over halibut. Bake for 20 minutes in 400-degree oven. Yield: 4 servings.

SNAPPY SNAPPER WITH DRESSING

1 c. bread crumbs
1/2 c. sherry
Butter
1/4 c. finely chopped green pepper
1/2 c. sliced mushrooms
1/2 c. finely chopped onion
2 tbsp. chopped parsley
1 2 to 3-lb. snapper
Olive oil
Paprika to taste
2 slices bacon
Hot water
Juice of 1/2 lemon

Soak bread crumbs in sherry. Saute in 3 tablespoons butter for 3 minutes, stirring constantly. Combine green pepper, mushrooms and onion. Add bread crumbs and parsley. Stuff snapper with dressing. Rub generously with olive oil and season with paprika. Place snapper in baking pan. Arrange bacon on top. Bake at 325 degrees for about 45 minutes, basting frequently with mixture of 2 parts hot water to 1 part butter and lemon juice. Yield: 4-6 servings.

BAKED SNAPPER WITH STUFFING

3/4 c. butter or margarine, melted
1/3 c. lemon juice
2 tsp. salt
1 6 to 10-lb. dressed snapper,
  flounder or grouper with head and tail
1 tsp. paprika

Mix butter, lemon juice and salt. Spoon over fish. Sprinkle with paprika. Seal securely in foil. Bake for 45 minutes at 350 degrees or until fish flakes easily.

Crab Meat Stuffing

1/2 c. chopped onion
1/3 c. chopped celery
1/3 c. chopped green pepper
2 cloves of minced garlic
1/2 c. butter or margarine, melted
2 c. bread crumbs
3 eggs
1 tbsp. chopped parsley
1 tsp. salt

1/2 tsp. pepper
1 lb. crab meat with bony bits removed

Cook onion, celery, green pepper and garlic in butter until vegetables are tender. Combine bread crumbs, eggs, parsley, salt and pepper. Add to vegetables. Combine vegetable mixture with crab meat; stuff fish.

WALNUT-STUFFED SOLE

1 1/2 c. chopped mushrooms
2 tbsp. chopped onions
2 tbsp. butter or margarine
1/2 c. finely chopped walnuts, toasted
1/4 c. chopped parsley
Salt to taste
1/8 tsp. dillweed (opt.)
6 fillets of sole
Juice of 1 lemon
Pepper
Mornay Sauce

Brown mushrooms and onions in butter in pan. Mix in walnuts, parsley, salt and dillweed. Sprinkle sole with lemon juice; season with salt and pepper to taste. Place 1 spoonful mushroom mixture on skin side of each fillet; roll up. Place in greased baking dish. Brush with additional melted butter. Bake at 350 degrees for 25 to 30 minutes or until fish flakes easily. Serve Mornay Sauce with baked sole.

Mornay Sauce

4 tbsp. butter
1 tbsp. finely chopped onion
3 tbsp. flour
3/4 c. cooled cooked chicken broth
1 c. cream
2 egg yolks
1/2 c. shredded Swiss cheese

Heat 3 tablespoons butter in heavy saucepan. Saute onion until tender. Blend in flour; heat until bubbly. Add broth and cream gradually, stirring. Bring to a boil rapidly, stirring constantly. Boil for 1 to 2 minutes. Blend several tablespoons hot mixture into egg yolks; return to hot mixture with cheese and remaining butter. Heat until cheese is melted.

Recipe for this photograph on page 60.

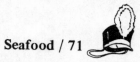

SALMON SONATA WITH LEMON SAUCE

1 c. chopped celery
1/2 c. chopped green pepper
6 c. bread cubes
1/2 c. stuffed olives, sliced
2 tbsp. chopped parsley
1/4 tsp. pepper
1 clove of garlic, minced
1 c. hot water
Salt
4 tbsp. lemon juice
Melted margarine
2 lb. salmon steak
Garlic salt to taste
Paprika to taste
2 egg yolks
1 1/2 c. medium white sauce

Mix first 8 ingredients with 1 tablespoon salt, 2 tablespoons lemon juice and 1/2 cup melted margarine. Place in shallow well-greased baking dish. Place salmon on top. Brush with additional margarine. Sprinkle with additional salt, garlic salt and paprika. Bake in 350-degree oven for 1 hour and 30 minutes. Add egg yolks and remaining lemon juice to white sauce. Serve over steaks. Garnish with parsley.

SALMON HOLLANDAISE IN SPINACH RING

1 1/2 c. bread crumbs
1/2 c. milk
1 tsp. grated onion
1 tbsp. melted butter
2 eggs, separated
5 c. cooked spinach
2 tbsp. lemon juice
Salt and pepper
4 c. salmon
Hollandaise sauce

Soak bread crumbs in milk; stir until smooth. Add onion, butter and egg yolks; mix well. Add finely chopped spinach seasoned with lemon juice, salt and pepper to taste. Fold in stiffly beaten egg whites. Turn into well-greased 10-inch ring mold. Bake at 350

Recipes for this photograph on page 72.

degrees for 40 minutes. Drain and flake salmon, reserving juice. Combine salmon and juice in double boiler; heat thoroughly. Loosen edge of spinach ring; turn out on hot serving plate. Fill center with hot drained salmon. Serve with hollandaise sauce.

SUPER SALMON LOAF

2 tbsp. butter
1/2 c. bread crumbs
1 1/2 c. milk
1 16-oz. can salmon, flaked
1 tbsp. chopped parsley
3 eggs
1 tsp. salt
1 tsp. pepper
1 tsp. paprika

Melt butter in saucepan; add bread crumbs and milk. Cook until crumbs are soft. Add remaining ingredients; mix lightly. Place in greased loaf pan. Bake in preheated 350-degree oven for 1 hour. Serve with cheese sauce or tartar sauce, if desired.

SALMON MOUNDS WITH CURRY SAUCE

1 sm. onion, minced
1/4 c. melted butter
Milk
1 1-lb. can salmon
3 c. soft bread crumbs
2 eggs
1/8 tsp. poultry seasoning
1/4 c. minced parsley
1/8 tsp. salt
Dash of nutmeg
1 can cream of mushroom soup
1/4 tsp. curry powder
1/4 tsp. paprika
2 stuffed olives, sliced

Cook onion in butter until golden. Drain salmon, reserving liquid. Add enough milk to liquid to equal 1/2 cup. Mix onion, salmon, liquid, crumbs, eggs, poultry seasoning, parsley, salt and nutmeg. Shape into 6 mounds in large shallow baking dish. Mix 1/2 cup milk, soup, curry powder and paprika. Pour around salmon. Top each salmon mound with olive slice. Bake, uncovered, in 350-degree oven about 45 minutes. Yield: 6 servings.

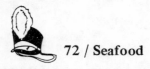

TUNA PIQUANT

    1   14-oz. box precooked rice
    2   sm. jars pimento, diced
    2   6-oz. cans tuna
    1   tsp. oregano
    1   sm. onion, diced
    1/2 tsp. garlic salt
    1   tsp. salt
    1   tbsp. caraway seed
    1/4 c. ripe olives, diced
    1/4 c. stuffed olives, sliced
    1   pkg. frozen mixed vegetables, thawed
    1/2 c. butter
    1   can mushroom soup
    1   c. milk
    1   c. grated Cheddar cheese
    1   tbsp. chives
    1   5-oz. package potato chips, broken

Combine first 11 ingredients; mix well. Place in large greased baking dish. Combine butter, soup, milk and cheese; heat slowly until cheese melts. Add chives. Pour over rice-tuna mixture. Bake for 30 minutes in 325-degree oven. Garnish with potato chips. Pimento pieces and green olive slices may be added for color. Yield: 10 servings.

TUNA COULIBIAC

    1/3 c. milk
    2   tbsp. butter or margarine
    2   tbsp. sugar
    1   tsp. salt
    1 1/2 tsp. active dry yeast
    2   tbsp. warm water
    1   egg, slightly beaten
    2 to 2 1/4 c. sifted all-purpose flour
    Rice Filling
    Tuna-Mushroom Filling
    1   egg
    2   tbsp. cream or evaporated milk

Heat milk, butter, sugar and salt in a saucepan until butter melts. Cool to lukewarm. Dissolve yeast in warm water. Add cooled milk mixture and egg. Beat in 1 3/4 to 2 cups flour to make a soft dough. Place dough on lightly floured surface. Knead in remaining flour; knead until dough is smooth, about 3 minutes. Shape into a ball. Place in greased bowl. Turn dough so greased side is up; cover. Let rise in warm place until doubled in bulk, about 1 hour and 30 minutes. Punch down dough; divide in two pieces, one piece slightly larger than the other. Roll smaller piece on floured surface into a 7 x 10-inch rectangle. Place on greased baking sheet. Spoon half the Rice Filling on rectangle, leaving a 1-inch border all around. Cover with Tuna-Mushroom Filling. Top with remaining Rice Filling. Beat 1 egg with cream. Brush border of dough with egg wash. Roll out remaining dough into 9 x 11-inch rectangle. Cut 11 x 2-inch strip for top braid; set aside. Place rectangle over filling; fold dough at corners into triangles to take up excess. Turn up bottom pastry against sides of loaf to form a seal with top pastry. Press indentations around the border every half-inch with the edge of a knife. Cut reserved strip of dough into 3 strips; braid. Brush egg wash down center of loaf. Press braid into place, tucking ends under loaf. Place in warm place to rise for 30 minutes. Make a hole in top of dough with greased funnel or aluminum cone to allow steam to escape. Cut 2 slits on either side of funnel. Bake loaf in 350-degree oven for 15 minutes. Brush loaf with egg wash. Bake 45 minutes longer, or until evenly browned. Cover braid with foil if it gets too brown. Cool on wire rack until ready to serve. Serve warm or at room temperature with sour cream or yogurt. Yield: 8 servings.

Rice Filling

    2   c. cooked rice
    1/4 c. each, finely chopped fresh
        parsley and dill
    1/2 tsp. salt

Mix rice, parsley, dill and salt in medium bowl. Two chopped, hard-cooked eggs may be added to rice mixture, if desired.

Tuna-Mushroom Filling

    2   tbsp. butter or margarine
    1/2 lb. mushrooms, finely chopped
    1/2 c. finely chopped scallions
    1/4 c. flour
    1   c. milk
    2   7-oz. cans tuna in vegetable oil
    1/4 tsp. salt
    1/8 tsp. each, nutmeg and pepper

Melt butter in skillet. Add mushrooms and scallions; cook over medium heat 5 minutes. Blend in flour; stir

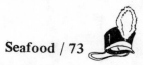

in milk. Cook, stirring, for 2 minutes longer. Stir in tuna and seasonings.

Photograph for this recipe on page 70.

VIENNA TUNA LOAF
WITH TOMATO SAUCE

3 2-oz. cans tuna in vegetable oil
2 eggs, beaten
1/2 c. sour cream
1 c. fresh bread crumbs
2 tbsp. finely chopped onion
1 tsp. salt
1/2 tsp. dried leaf thyme
1/4 c. sliced pimento-stuffed olives
3 hard-cooked eggs
Tomato Sauce

Break tuna into flakes in bowl. Stir in eggs, sour cream, bread crumbs, onion, salt and thyme. Line a 4-cup loaf pan with greased foil. Arrange olives on bottom. Gently spoon in half the tuna mixture, making a trough down the middle with back of tablespoon. Place eggs lengthwise in trough. Top with remaining tuna mixture. Shape into loaf. Bake in 375-degree oven for 45 minutes. Unmold onto hot platter. Serve with Tomato Sauce. Yield: 6 servings.

Tomato Sauce

2 tbsp. butter
2 tbsp. olive oil
1 c. chopped onions
1 clove of garlic, minced
1 1-lb. 12-oz. can Italian plum tomatoes
1 tsp. salt
1/2 tsp. sugar
1/2 tsp. dried leaf thyme
1/2 tsp. dried leaf marjoram

Heat butter and oil in a large skillet. Add onions and garlic; cook until tender. Stir in tomatoes, salt, sugar, thyme and marjoram. Simmer, uncovered, 20 minutes. Put through a food mill or puree in blender. Simmer, uncovered, 20 minutes or until thickened.

Photograph for this recipe on page 70.

SEAFOOD GUMBO SERENADE

Cooking oil
2 to 3 tbsp. flour
1 lg. onion, diced
1/2 c. diced celery
1/4 c. diced bell pepper
2 qt. boiling water or chicken broth
1 lb. fresh shrimp, cleaned
1 bay leaf
1/2 lb. crab meat
2 c. oysters
Salt and pepper to taste
Steamed rice
File powder

Heat enough oil in heavy pot to cover bottom. Add flour; cook, stirring, until blended. Cook over low heat, stirring constantly, until flour is dark brown. Add onion, celery and bell pepper; cook over low heat, stirring, until onion is wilted, not brown. Add boiling water. Add shrimp and bay leaf. Simmer for 1 hour, stirring occasionally. Add crab meat and oysters. Simmer for 15 minutes longer. Add salt and pepper. Serve in soup tureen with large bowl of rice. Place mound of rice in each soup bowl; ladle in gumbo. Place pinch of file powder in each serving.

MOLDED SALAD NOCTURNE

    1 tbsp. unflavored gelatin
    1/4 c. cold water
    3/4 c. chili sauce
    2 c. cottage cheese
    1 c. sour cream
    1/2 tsp. prepared mustard
    1/2 tsp. sugar
    1/4 tsp. salt
    1   7-oz. can tuna, drained
    1/2 c. finely chopped celery
    1/4 c. sliced green onions

Soften gelatin in water. Heat chili sauce to boiling in saucepan; add gelatin. Stir until dissolved; set aside. Combine cottage cheese, sour cream, mustard, sugar and salt in large bowl; stir until blended. Fold in tuna, celery, onions and chili sauce. Pour into a 6-cup mold. Chill until firm. Unmold onto chilled plate. Surround with tomatoes and green pepper strips. Yield: 8 servings.

TUNA BAKE WITH BISCUIT TOPPING

    3 tbsp. chopped onion
    1/3 c. chopped green pepper
    3 tbsp. fat
    1/2 tsp. salt
    6 tbsp. flour
    1   10 1/2-oz. can mushroom soup
    1 1/2 c. milk
    1   7-oz. can tuna
    1 1/2 tbsp. lemon juice
    Canned biscuits

Brown onion and green pepper in hot fat. Add salt and flour, blending well. Add soup and milk. Cook until sauce is thick and smooth. Add tuna chunks and lemon juice. Pour into greased 10-inch pan. Cover with canned biscuits. Bake at 450 degrees for 12 to 15 minutes. Yield: 5-6 servings.

TWO-WAY TUNA

    1/4 c. mayonnaise
    1 tbsp. minced onion
    1 tsp. lemon juice
    1 tsp. soy sauce
    1/2 tsp. curry powder (opt.)
    1   7-oz. can tuna, flaked
    1   5-oz. can sliced water chestnuts,
        drained
    6 to 8 thin slices French bread

Combine mayonnaise, onion, lemon juice, soy sauce and curry powder; blend well. Add tuna and water chestnuts; toss gently. Spread tuna mixture on bread slices. Broil 2 to 3 inches from heat for 3 to 4 minutes or until hot. May chill tuna mixture and serve in lettuce cups. Homemade bread may be substituted for French bread. Yield: 6-8 servings.

TUNA WITH CURRIED ALMOND-RICE

    1 c. rice
    8 tbsp. butter
    1 can whole tomatoes, drained and
        chopped
    1 clove of garlic, minced
    1 tsp. Worcestershire sauce
    4 drops of Tabasco sauce
    1 tbsp. chopped parsley
    1/4 tsp. paprika
    1 tsp. salt
    Dash of pepper
    6 tbsp. flour
    2 c. milk
    1/2 c. white wine
    2   9 1/4-oz. cans tuna, drained and
        rinsed
    1/2 tsp. curry powder
    1 c. blanched almonds

Place rice and 2 cups water in casserole; cover. Bake in preheated 350-degree oven for 1 hour. Melt 6 tablespoons butter in top of double boiler. Add tomatoes, garlic, Worcestershire sauce, Tabasco sauce, parsley, paprika, salt and pepper. Simmer, covered, for several minutes. Add flour; blend well. Add milk; cook, stirring constantly, until thickened. Add wine and tuna. Keep warm over simmering water. Melt remaining butter in small frypan. Add curry powder and almonds. Cook over low heat, stirring, until almonds are brown. Stir into rice. Serve tuna mixture over rice. Yield: 6 servings.

SEAFOOD OPERETTA

1 can artichoke hearts
2 lb. shrimp, cooked
2 tbsp. butter
3 tbsp. flour
1/4 tsp. red pepper
1/4 tsp. paprika
1 tsp. salt
1 pt. half and half
1 tsp. Worcestershire sauce
1 tbsp. catsup
1 tsp. lemon juice
2 tbsp. sherry

Cut artichoke hearts in thin slices; drain for 1 hour. Alternate layers of shrimp and artichoke hearts in casserole. Melt butter in saucepan. Add flour, pepper, paprika and salt, stirring until blended. Add half and half gradually; cook, stirring constantly, until thickened. Add Worcestershire sauce, catsup, lemon juice and sherry. Pour over shrimp and artichoke hearts. Bake at 325 degrees for about 30 minutes.

PICKLED SHRIMP BOOGIE

2 1/2 lb. shrimp, cooked
3 med. onions, sliced
7 bay leaves
1 1/4 c. salad oil
3/4 c. white vinegar
1 1/2 tsp. salt
2 1/2 tsp. celery seed
2 1/2 tsp. juice of capers
Dash of hot sauce

Alternate layers of shrimp and onions in bowl. Spread bay leaves over shrimp mixture. Mix all remaining ingredients. Pour over shrimp mixture. Refrigerate for 24 hours, tossing occasionally. Add pepper, horseradish and paprika, if desired. Yield: 6 servings.

SAVORY SEAFOOD

1 lb. peeled shrimp
1 lb. crab meat
1 1/2 to 2 c. finely diced celery
1/2 to 1 c. diced green pepper
1/4 c. diced onion
1 c. mayonnaise
1 tsp. salt
1 tbsp. Worcestershire sauce
2 c. crushed potato chips

Combine seafood, vegetables, mayonnaise, salt and Worcestershire sauce, blending well. Spoon into 9 x 13-inch baking dish. Sprinkle with potato chips. Bake in a 400-degree oven for 20 to 25 minutes. Yield 4-6 servings.

HOT CLAM DIP

1 8-oz. package cream cheese
1 can minced clams
2 tbsp. margarine
2 tbsp. sherry or bourbon
1/2 tsp. curry powder
1/2 tsp. confectioners' sugar
1 clove of garlic, minced
1 sm. onion, grated
Chopped chives or parsley

Soften cream cheese; stir in clams and liquid. Add remaining ingredients except chives; mix well. Place in buttered small baking dish. Sprinkle with chives. Bake in preheated 325-degree oven for 30 minutes. Cool for 10 minutes to thicken before serving. Serve with crackers.

CLAM CHOWDER CONCERTO

5 slices bacon, finely chopped
1/4 c. chopped onion
2 c. cubed potatoes
2 c. clam juice and water
2 c. minced clams, drained
3 tbsp. melted margarine
3 tbsp. flour
1/4 tsp. salt
Dash of pepper
4 c. milk, scalded

Brown bacon in skillet. Add onion; cook until clear. Add potatoes and 2 cups liquid; cover. Bring to a boil. Simmer for 15 minutes; add clams. Blend margarine, flour, salt and pepper; add milk slowly. Cook until thickened, stirring constantly. Add to clam mixture. Season to taste. Simmer, covered, for 10 minutes or longer. Yield: 4 servings.

BAKED STUFFED CLAMS

2 cans minced clams
1 c. packaged corn bread stuffing
3 drops of Tabasco sauce
1/2 c. finely chopped celery
2 tbsp. finely chopped onion
2 tbsp. finely chopped green pepper
Salt and pepper to taste

Drain clams; reserve liquid. Combine clams with remaining ingredients, adding enough reserved liquid to moisten well. Place in baking shells on a baking sheet. Bake in preheated 350-degree oven for 10 to 15 minutes or until brown. Garnish each shell with thin wedge of lemon.

CRAB MEAT-BACON ROLLS

1/2 c. tomato juice
1 egg, well beaten
1 c. dry bread crumbs
1/8 tsp. salt
1/8 tsp. garlic powder
Dash of freshly ground pepper
1/2 tsp. chopped parsley
1/2 tsp. chopped celery leaves
1 6 1/2-oz. can crab meat, flaked
12 slices bacon, cut in half

Mix tomato juice and egg; Add crumbs, seasonings, parsley, celery leaves and crab meat; mix thoroughly. Shape into finger lengths. Wrap each roll with 1/2 slice bacon; fasten with toothpick. Place in baking pan. Broil, turning frequently, until browned evenly. Yield: 2 dozen rolls.

CRAB LOUIS MOLD

2 env. plain gelatin
1 c. cold water
2/3 c. chili sauce

1/2 c. rose wine
1/2 c. thick sour cream
1/2 c. mayonnaise
1/2 c. tomato juice
1 tbsp. instant minced onion
1 tbsp. lime or lemon juice
1/2 tsp. salt
1/2 c. ripe olives
4 hard-boiled eggs
1 1/2 c. crab meat
Salad greens

Soften gelatin in 1/2 cup water. Heat remaining water with chili sauce. Dissolve gelatin in hot chili sauce. Add wine, sour cream, mayonnaise, tomato juice, minced onion, lime juice and salt. Chill until mixture is partially set. Cut part of olives into wedges, reserving remaining olives for garnish. Chop 2 eggs. Fold crab meat, olives and chopped eggs into gelatin mixture. Chill until firm. Unmold on salad greens. Cut remaining eggs into wedges. Garnish salad with eggs and remaining olives. Yield: 8 servings.

CRAB CAKES CADENZA

1 lb. fresh crab meat
Salt to taste
1 tbsp. chopped parsley
Juice of 1/2 lemon
1 egg
1 1/2 slices bread, crumbled
1 tbsp. Worcestershire sauce
1 tsp. mustard
Dash of hot sauce
Butter or oil

Break up crab meat in large bowl. Sprinkle with salt, parsley and lemon juice; blend well. Beat egg slightly with fork in small bowl; add bread crumbs, Worcestershire sauce, mustard and hot sauce. Mix well. Add small amount of milk to thoroughly moisten mixture, if desired. Pour egg mixture over crab meat; blend well. Pat into 8 cakes. Saute each cake on both sides in butter over moderate heat until golden brown. Yield: 4 servings.

LOBSTER-ARTICHOKE SALAD

1 c. chopped lobster
1 pkg. long grain and wild rice, cooked

1/2 green pepper, diced
12 black olives, sliced
2 6-oz. jars marinated artichoke hearts
2 sweet cherry peppers, sliced or chopped
1/2 c. mayonnaise
2 tbsp. vinegar
1/4 tsp. dry mustard
3/4 tsp. curry powder

Mix lobster with rice. Add green pepper, olives, artichoke hearts and cherry peppers; toss well. Blend remaining ingredients; mix with rice mixture. Chill for several hours. Crab, ham, chicken or shrimp may be substituted for lobster.

BAKED STUFFED LOBSTER POLKA

1 1 to 1 1/4-lb. lobster, cooked and
   halved
1 to 1 1/2 lb. fresh shrimp
Flavored bread crumbs
Butter

Clean lobster and shrimp. Boil shrimp in water to cover for 5 minutes or until pink. Remove shrimp from water; reserve water. Saute bread crumbs in small amount of butter until browned. Cut shrimp in small pieces; stir into bread crumbs. Add 1/2 cup reserved shrimp water. Toss to moisten bread crumbs. Mound shrimp stuffing over lobster halves. Place in shallow baking dish. Bake in 350-degree oven for 25 to 30 minutes or until heated through.

LOBSTER A LA NEWBURG IN RAGTIME

2 lb. cooked lobster, sliced
1/4 c. melted butter
3 tbsp. sherry
2 tbsp. brandy
1/3 c. heavy cream
Salt and cayenne pepper to taste
Dash of nutmeg
2 egg yolks, well beaten

Cook lobster in butter over low heat for 3 minutes. Add sherry and brandy; cook for 1 minute. Add cream and seasonings. Stir in egg yolks; cook, stirring, until thickened. Serve on toast. Yield: 4 servings.

FRENCH-FRIED OYSTERS ALLEGRO

Salt and pepper to taste
1 lg. can fresh oysters
2 c. flour
2 c. buttermilk
2 c. cracker meal

Salt and pepper oysters. Dip in flour, then buttermilk. Roll in cracker meal. Drop in deep fat; fry until golden brown. Drain on paper. Yield: 4 servings.

OYSTERS BIENVILLE

1 bunch green onions and tops, minced
2 tbsp. butter
2 tbsp. flour
2/3 c. chicken broth
1/3 c. mushroom pieces
1 egg yolk
1/3 c. white wine
1 tsp. salt
Dash of cayenne pepper
2 doz. oysters
1/2 c. French bread crumbs
1 tbsp. Parmesan cheese

Saute onions and tops in butter in a skillet over low heat about 6 minutes or until tender. Add flour; cook until brown. Stir in chicken broth and mushrooms. Beat egg yolk with wine; slowly add to sauce, beating rapidly. Season with salt and cayenne pepper. Cook for 10 to 15 minutes over low heat, stirring constantly. Drain oysters; place 1 on each half shell. Set shells on pan of ice cream salt which has been heated in 400-degree oven for 30 minutes. Bake for 5 minutes. Pour sauce over each oyster. Sprinkle with combined bread crumbs and cheese. Return to oven. Bake for about 15 minutes or until lightly browned. Yield: 4 servings.

OYSTERS ROCKEFELLER

8 tbsp. butter
5 tbsp. finely minced spinach
2 tbsp. finely minced onion
1 1/2 tbsp. minced cooked lettuce
2 tsp. minced celery

3 tbsp. fine dry crumbs
1 tsp. each minced fresh chervil and
*   tarragon*
1/4 tsp. anchovy paste
Dash of pepper
1/4 tsp. salt
Dash of hot sauce
Dash of absinthe
24 oysters on the half shell

Heat butter. Add spinach, onion, lettuce, celery, crumbs, herbs, anchovy paste, pepper and salt. Add hot sauce and absinthe. Remove oysters from shells; scrub shells. Boil to be sure every particle of sand has been washed away. Place 6 shells on each of 4 pie plates holding hot rock salt. Place 1 oyster in each shell. Broil slowly for 5 minutes. Place 1 spoonful spinach mixture on each oyster. Broil until thoroughly heated. Serve immediately. Yield: 4 servings.

OLIVE-SHRIMP TREE WITH SPANISH SAUCE

4 lb. medium shrimp
1   12-in. styrofoam cone
Wide mesh screening
Pins or staples

2 bunches parsley
2 1/2 c. pimento-stuffed olives
Spanish Sauce

Cook shrimp in boiling salted water for about 3 to 5 minutes; peel and devein. Cover styrofoam cone with screening. Fasten with pins. Separate parsley into individual sprigs; insert stems in screening. Cover entire cone with parsley sprigs. Insert wooden picks in vertical rows in cone, spacing picks about 1 inch apart. Place 1 shrimp, curved side up, on each pick. Place additional pick in curve of each shrimp; fasten olive on each pick. Top cone with additional stuffed olive; surround with parsley sprigs. Sprinkle or spray entire surface lightly with water; cover with plastic wrap. Chill until serving time. Serve with Spanish Sauce as dip.

Spanish Sauce

1 c. mayonnaise
1/2 c. catsup
1/4 c. chili sauce
1/2 c. chopped pimento-stuffed olives
1 1/2 tbsp. brandy
1/2 tsp. Dijan mustard
1/2 tsp. Worcestershire sauce
1/2 tsp. curry powder
1/2 tsp. paprika
1/2 tsp. lemon juice
Dash of coarsely ground pepper

Blend mayonnaise, catsup, chili sauce and olives together. Stir in brandy. Add remaining ingredients, blending well. Chill.

Photograph for this recipe on page 66.

FRENCH-MARINATED SHRIMP

1 can tomato soup
3/4 c. sugar
1 c. oil
1 tsp. salt
3/4 c. vinegar
2 tbsp. Worcestershire sauce
1 tsp. pepper
1 tbsp. paprika
1 sm. onion, grated
1 tbsp. prepared mustard
1 clove of garlic, cut in half
1 sm. green pepper, chopped

2 or 3 oranges, chopped
1 to 2 lb. cleaned cooked shrimp

Make dressing of first 11 ingredients; chill overnight. Add green pepper and oranges. Cut shrimp into bite-sized pieces. Stir into dressing mixture. Chill for 4 to 5 hours. Remove garlic before serving.

SHRIMP REMOULADE

1/2 c. tarragon vinegar
4 tbsp. horseradish or horseradish mustard
1 tsp. salt
1/2 tsp. cayenne pepper
1 tbsp. paprika
2 tbsp. catsup
1 c. salad oil
1 clove of garlic, finely minced
1/2 c. finely minced shallots
1/2 c. finely minced celery
Boiled shrimp or lump crab meat

Mix vinegar, horseradish, salt, cayenne pepper, paprika and catsup thoroughly. Add oil slowly, beating constantly. Add garlic, shallots and celery; mix thoroughly. Marinate shrimp for several hours before serving. Serve on shredded lettuce with additional sauce.

SHRIMP IN DOUBLE TIME

1/4 c. oil
2 c. sliced onions
1 tsp. saffron
3/4 tbsp. chili powder
1/2 c. chopped onion
2 tbsp. minced garlic
1 tbsp. ginger
1 1/2 tsp. salt
2 lb. shelled shrimp, deveined
2 c. sour cream

Heat oil in skillet. Saute onions until browned lightly. Add saffron, chili powder, chopped onion, garlic, ginger, salt and shrimp; mix well. Cook over low heat for 6 minutes. Stir in sour cream. Cook until heated through, but do not boil. Serve with rice. Yield: 4 servings.

Outdoor Meats In Tempo

Mealtime becomes a special treat for mom when the grill is prepared for a cookout, because that is when dad and the kids take over, with dad dressed in his special garb, tongs in hand, looking like a conductor ready to lead the music. Cookout time is masterpiece time, because there is hardly any meat — beef, lamb, fish, seafood, poultry and pork all included — whose flavor doesn't harmonize perfectly with the aroma of a charcoal fire. Cooking over an outdoor fire or on a spit was, of course, a very early form of cooking; there was no other way. Today, despite the ease and exactness of electric and gas ranges, microwave ovens, and other modern appliances, families continue cooking meats over a barbecue grill. There is just no substitute, not even the best "hickory-flavored barbecue sauce," for the flavor that a charcoal grill or wood fire imparts to food. If you know how to start a fire, you can cook almost anywhere, almost any time — even during a power failure! Fresh-caught fish and shellfish become a sizzling gourmet treat when cooked over a fire on the beach. On a grill at a lakeside cabin, or over a campfire by a tent in the woods, trout, salmon, and other fresh-water fish are an incomparable way to satisfy an appetite. Don't limit your outdoor cooking to the outdoors! On rainy days or cold winter evenings, cook your hamburgers, chicken, steaks, or ribs over a charcoal fire built right in your fireplace.

The kids always like to help with outdoor cookouts, especially when you've planned *Stuffed Whopper Burgers* as the star attraction. When the supermarket features a Saturday special on broilers, serve *Chili-Barbecued Chicken* to the family on Sunday. Try *Saucy Lobster Grill,* or *Patio Grilled Trout,* and you'll feature grilled fish and shellfish as the mealtime high note all the time.

Mouthwatering recipes galore, that's what you'll find in this section on Outdoor Meats!

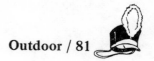

CHARCOALING — BY THE RULES

HOW TO LIGHT THE FIRE — THE RIGHT WAY

Every successful cookout begins with a good fire.

1. Line the grill with heavy duty aluminum foil — for faster cooking and easier clean-up later.

2. Stack the briquets in a pyramid; they'll light faster since air can circulate around them.

3. Use a good starter. Try the electric or chimney type, or choose a liquid, jelly or solid fibrous cubes.

4. Be patient! Let the briquets burn to just the right stage before adding food. Generally they'll require 20 to 40 minutes.

HOW TO JUDGE THE TEMPERATURE OF A CHARCOAL BRIQUET FIRE

- *To tell when it's cooking time:* Different brands of charcoal give off varying degrees of heat in a given time . . . thus some are ready for cooking sooner than others. In daylight, the coals are ready for cooking when they are covered by a layer of gray ash; at night they'll have a bright red glow. At this stage, spread the briquets into a single layer with tongs and place food on the grill.

- *Quick temperature test:* Hold your hand at the cooking height, palm side down. If you can keep it in position for 2 seconds, the temperature is high or hot; 3 seconds, medium-high or hot; 4 seconds, medium; 5 seconds, low.

- *To lower the temperature:* Raise the grid, or spread out the coals.

- *To raise the temperature:* Tap ash from coals, or push them closer.

- *When more coals are needed:* Add to the outer edge of hot coals.

- *If spattering fat causes flare-ups:* Put flames out by raising grid, spreading out coals, or removing a few coals. If all else fails, have a water bottle handy (remove food before sprinkling). For rotisserie cooking, place foil drip pan in front of the coals in the fire box to catch the drippings, thus eliminating flare-ups before they start.

HOW TO MAKE CLEAN-UP EASY

- *Prevention:* Line the grill with heavy duty aluminum foil . . . spray the grill rack with a non-stick coating.

- *Cure:* To remove grease and grilled-on food particles, sprinkle dry baking soda on a damp sponge and scour; rinse with water/soda solution.

- *Store:* Clean after each use; then cover the grill and store in a clean, dry place.

INSTRUMENTAL STEW

15 potatoes, peeled
5 carrots, peeled
3 onions, peeled
1 1/2 lb. ground beef
Salt and pepper

Slice potatoes, carrots and onions. Place in large bowl; cover with water. Grease squares of foil. Shape beef into patties; place one on each square of foil. Drain vegetables thoroughly. Top ground beef with vegetables. Season with salt and pepper. Fold foil; seal well. Place on outdoor grill. Cook for 30 minutes; turn foil package over. Cook until beef and vegetables are tender.

COFFEE CAN COMPOSITION

1 1/2 lb. ground beef
2 med. onions, sliced
3 med. potatoes, thinly sliced
4 carrots, thinly sliced
Butter
Salt to taste
Pepper to taste

Spread beef in large coffee can. Place layer of onions on ground beef. Top onions with layer of potatoes and layer of carrots. Repeat until all vegetables are used. Dot with butter. Season with salt and pepper; cover. Place on rack over hot coals. Cook until ground beef and vegetables are tender. Yield: 6-8 servings.

HOBO DINNER HARMONICA

2/3 c. ground beef
Salt and pepper to taste
2 tbsp. chopped onion
1 carrot, cut into strips
1 sm. onion
1 sm. potato, quartered
1/2 ear corn
1/4 c. chopped ripe olives

Combine beef with salt, pepper and chopped onion. Pat to fit bottom of small coffee can. Place carrot strips, onion, potato and corn over beef. Sprinkle with salt, pepper and olives. Cover. Cook over medium-hot coals for 50 minutes. Yield: 1 serving.

PICNIC KABOBS

1 1/2 lb. ground beef
1 c. oats
1 egg, beaten
1 tsp. salt
1 tbsp. Worcestershire sauce
1/4 c. tomato sauce
24 med. stuffed olives
4 med. tomatoes
2 green peppers
8 sm. whole cooked potatoes
8 button mushrooms
Barbecue sauce

Combine ground beef, oats, egg, salt, Worcestershire sauce and tomato sauce. Shape small amount of ground beef mixture around each olive. Cut tomatoes and green peppers into eighths; seed peppers. Alternate 3 meatballs, 2 tomato wedges, 2 green pepper pieces, 1 potato and 1 mushroom on eight 12-inch metal skewers. Brush with barbecue sauce. Broil kabobs over coals, 6 inches from source of heat, for 8 to 10 minutes. Turn and baste frequently with barbecue sauce.

BEEFBURGER HULA

1 lb. ground beef
1/2 tsp. salt
1 onion, chopped fine
1/2 c. soy sauce
1 sm. clove of garlic, minced
1/2 tsp. ground ginger

Combine beef, salt and onion. Shape into 6 patties. Combine soy sauce, garlic and ginger. Pour over patties. Marinate patties in sauce for at least 30 minutes. Remove from sauce. Broil, over hot coals 4 to 5 inches from source of heat, for 5 to 7 minutes on each side.

WHOPPER BURGER IN
WALTZ-TIME

2 lb. ground beef
1 tsp. salt
Pepper to taste
1 tbsp. Worcestershire sauce
1 egg

American cheese slices
1 onion, sliced
Mustard relish
Barbecue sauce

Combine beef, seasonings and egg. Shape into thin patties. Place 1 slice cheese, 1 slice onion and 1 teaspoon mustard relish on half the patties. Top with remaining patties, sealing edges well. Cook on outdoor grill, basting with barbecue sauce. Yield: 6-8 servings.

BLUE CHEESE PATTIES

2 oz. blue cheese
1 onion, chopped
2 tbsp. chopped parsley
2 eggs
2 tbsp. cream
2 tbsp. catsup
1 clove of garlic, halved
1 lb. ground beef

Combine blue cheese, onion, parsley, eggs, cream, catsup and garlic in blender container. Blend until mixture is pureed. Pour blue cheese mixture over beef; mix well. Shape into patties. Broil over hot coals on barbecue grill.

POOR MAN'S GRILLED STEAK

1 round French bread loaf
1/2 tsp. prepared mustard
1/2 tsp. chili powder
1/2 c. soft butter
3 lb. ground chuck
2 tsp. seasoned salt
1/2 c. minced green onions and tops
2 tbsp. chili sauce
1 tbsp. soy sauce
1 cucumber
1 tomato

Cut bread in halves crosswise. Blend mustard, chili powder and butter. Spread over cut sides of bread. Combine ground beef, seasoned salt, green onions, chili sauce and soy sauce; blend well. Form beef mixture into 2 patties slightly larger than cut side of bread. Place bread, crust down, on grill away from hottest coals to heat slowly. Grill patties on one side

until browned; turn patties. Place bread on patties. Cook until patties are browned and tender. Arrange on platter. Cut cucumber and tomato into halves; slice thinly. Arrange on patties. Cut each round into 5 wedges to serve.

PATIO PATTIES

2 lb. ground beef
2 tsp. salt
1/2 tsp. pepper
1 c. whole cranberry sauce
1/4 c. sliced stuffed olives
1/4 c. thinly sliced celery
1 tsp. lemon juice
1 tsp. chopped onion

Combine beef, salt and pepper. Shape into 8 patties. Place patties on grill over glowing coals, about 3 inches from heat. Grill for about 10 minutes; turn. Grill for 5 minutes longer or until of desired doneness.

MOCK FILET MIGNON

1 lb. ground beef
1 tbsp. Worcestershire sauce
1 tsp. dried minced onion
1/4 c. catsup
1 tsp. garlic juice
Salt and pepper to taste
4 slices bacon

Combine all ingredients except bacon. Shape into 4 patties. Wrap 1 slice of bacon around each patty. Secure with toothpick. Broil over hot coals, 4 to 5 inches from source of heat, for 7 minutes on each side or until of desired doneness.

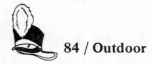
BROILED TENDERLOIN KABOBS

2 c. oil
2 c. red wine vinegar
1/2 tsp. pickling spices
2 lb. beef tenderloin tips
5 sm. white onions
2 bell peppers
10 mushroom caps
5 cherry tomatoes

Combine oil, vinegar, pickling spices and beef tips. Marinate for 24 hours. Parboil onions and bell peppers. Let cool. Cut onions in half. Cut bell peppers in 1-inch square pieces. Prepare 5 kabob skewers, starting with 1 mushroom on each skewer. Add a beef tip, onion half, bell pepper square, beef tip, tomato, beef tip, onion half, bell pepper square, beef tip and end with a mushroom. Charcoal broil kabobs to desired doneness.

CHATEAUBRIAND ENSEMBLE

1   2-in. thick round steak
1/2 tsp. monosodium glutamate
1 c. tomato sauce
1 tbsp. brown sugar
1 tsp. tenderizer
1/4 c. butter or margarine
1 to 2 tbsp. prepared mustard
1 tbsp. Worcestershire sauce
1 clove of garlic, minced
1/4 c. chopped parsley
1/2 to 1 c. dry red wine

Pierce steak deeply with fork. Sprinkle each side with monosodium glutamate. Allow to stand for 1 hour before cooking. Combine remaining ingredients except wine in saucepan, stirring until sauce comes to a slow boil. Lower heat; simmer for 5 minutes. Add wine; set aside until ready to use. Place steak on grill 2 inches above coals. Slash fatty edges on steak; brush with sauce. Sear steak quickly on each side. Raise grill; cook, basting occasionally, to desired doneness. Slice diagonally. Yield: 8 servings.

STEAK SONATA

2 1/2 tbsp. (packed) brown sugar
1 1/2 tbsp. sugar
1 tbsp. ground ginger
1 clove of garlic, crushed
1/2 c. soy sauce
1 tbsp. tarragon vinegar
3 lb. rib steaks, 1 1/2 in. thick

Blend all ingredients except steaks. Place steaks in large shallow dish. Pour sauce over top. Marinate for at least 30 minutes, basting frequently and turning once or twice. Remove steaks from marinade, reserving marinade. Place steaks on grill about 3 inches from coals. Grill for 6 minutes or until one side is browned, brushing frequently with marinade. Turn and grill other side for 6 minutes or until done. Serve immediately. Yield: 6 servings.

CHARCOALED TERIYAKI STEAK

1   2-lb. flank steak
1/2 c. sugar
1 tsp. sesame seed
Dash of salt
1/2 c. soy sauce
1 tsp. vinegar
1 tsp. ginger
2 cloves of garlic, crushed

Trim steak, removing all fibers. Cut steak crosswise in medium-thick slices. Mix sugar, sesame seed, salt, soy sauce, vinegar, ginger and garlic to make marinade. Place steak in marinade. Let stand for at least 2 hours. Drain steak. Grill over hot coals to desired doneness. Serve on toasted buns, if desired. Yield: 8 servings.

STRIP STEAK SYMPHONY

3 lg. red onions, sliced
1 c. butter
4 tsp. salt
1/2 tsp. freshly ground pepper
4 tsp. dry mustard
4 tsp. Worcestershire sauce
4 tbsp. red table wine
1   6-lb. New York strip steak

Place half the onions on piece of wide foil. Dot onions with 1/2 cup butter. Add salt, pepper and mustard. Pour Worcestershire sauce over mixture. Pour 2 tablespoons wine on one side of steak. Turn; add remaining wine. Place steak on top of butter and onions. Place remaining onions and butter over steak. Fold foil and seal edges. Seal in 2 more pieces of foil. Cook on grill for about 45 minutes. Remove steak from foil. Place over charcoal for about 8 minutes on each side. Serve onions and juice in bowl.

OVER-THE-COALS CHUCK STEAK

1/2 c. salad oil
1/3 c. cider vinegar
1/3 c. chopped onion
1 tsp. salt
Dash of pepper
2 tbsp. steak sauce
1 lg. chuck steak

Combine oil, vinegar, onion, salt, pepper and steak sauce for marinade. Marinate steak in sauce for at least 1 hour at room temperature. Cook on grill over hot coals to desired doneness. Yield: 5-6 servings.

FLANK STEAK A LA BLUE

1/3 c. white wine vinegar
1/3 c. water
2 tbsp. soy sauce
1 med. onion, sliced
1 clove of garlic, sliced
Freshly ground pepper
1 1/2 to 2 lb. flank steak, scored
1/4 c. crumbled Blue cheese

Combine vinegar, water, soy sauce, onion, garlic and pepper in shallow dish. Marinate steak at least 6 hours, turning occasionally. Place steak 4 to 5 inches from coals. Broil 5 to 7 minutes. Turn; sprinkle with Blue cheese. Continue to broil to desired degree of doneness. Place on serving platter. Slice in thin diagonal slices across grain. Yield: 6 servings.

FUDGE-FROSTED PEANUT BUTTER CAKE

3/4 c. butter
3/4 c. creamy peanut butter
2 c. (firmly packed) light brown sugar
1 tsp. vanilla
3 eggs
2 c. all-purpose flour
1 tbsp. baking powder
1/2 tsp. salt
1 c. milk
1 pkg. semisweet chocolate pieces
1/3 c. evaporated milk
1 1/2 c. confectioners' sugar
1/2 c. chopped peanuts

Cream together butter and peanut butter in large mixing bowl. Add sugar; beat thoroughly. Add vanilla. Beat in eggs, one at a time. Sift together flour, baking powder and salt. Add to creamed mixture alternately with milk. Turn into pan. Bake in preheated 350-degree oven for 45 to 50 minutes. Cool on wire rack. Heat chocolate pieces in evaporated milk over very low heat, stirring constantly, until mixture is smooth and thick. Remove from heat; stir in sugar until smooth. Spread on cake. Sprinkle with peanuts. If frosting becomes too stiff, add more evaporated milk.

Photograph for these recipes on page 88.

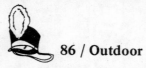
PAN-AMERICAN STEAK

1/2 c. butter
Juice of 2 limes
1 tsp. garlic powder
1/2 c. Burgundy
1 tbsp. Worcestershire sauce
1 tsp. soy sauce
1 tsp. monosodium glutamate
1 tsp. hot sauce
Salt and pepper to taste
1   3-lb. porterhouse steak, 2 in. thick

Combine butter, lime juice, garlic powder, Burgundy, Worcestershire sauce, soy sauce, monosodium glutamate, hot sauce, salt and pepper in saucepan. Simmer for 3 minutes. Pour over steak. Marinate for at least 2 hours, turning steak every 15 minutes. Cook over hickory chips and charcoal to desired degree of doneness. Baste frequently with marinade. Yield: 4 servings.

MARINATED FLANK STEAK

1/4 c. soy sauce
3 tbsp. honey
2 tbsp. vinegar
1 1/2 tsp. garlic powder
1 1/2 tsp. ginger
3/4 c. salad oil
1 green onion, minced
1   1 1/2-lb. flank steak

Mix soy sauce, honey and vinegar; blend in garlic powder and ginger. Add oil and green onion. Place steak in shallow pan. Cover with marinade. Let stand for at least 4 hours. Cook steak on grill for 5 minutes on each side for medium rare, basting occasionally with marinade. Yield: 4 servings.

BARBECUED HAM SLICES

1 c. (firmly packed) brown sugar
3 tbsp. catsup
1 tbsp. soy sauce
1 tsp. dry mustard
2 tbsp. green pepper flakes
1 c. crushed pineapple

1 1/2 tbsp. cornstarch
3/4 to 1-in. thick ready-to-eat ham slices

Combine 1 cup water and brown sugar in saucepan. Add catsup, soy sauce, mustard, pepper flakes and pineapple. Bring to a boil. Simmer for 10 minutes. Dissolve cornstarch in 1/4 cup cold water; add to sauce. Cook, stirring, until sauce is clear and thickened. Cook ham on grill over hot coals for about 8 minutes; baste frequently with sauce. Serve with additional sauce.

BROILED PORK CHOPS IN MARINADE

1 onion, minced
1 clove of garlic, chopped
1/2 c. soy sauce
2/3 c. water
1 tbsp. ginger
3 tbsp. sugar
8 pork chops, cut 2 in. thick

Combine first 6 ingredients for marinade. Place chops in marinade for at least 10 hours. Cook on outdoor grill until done. Yield: 8 servings.

FRANK KABOBS

1/3 c. (packed) brown sugar
1/2 tsp. nutmeg
2 tbsp. orange juice
6 tbsp. melted butter
4 onions
4 apples
1 lb. frankfurters
2 apple slices

Combine brown sugar, nutmeg, orange juice and butter for basting sauce. Parboil onions; cut in thick slices. Cut apples in thick slices. Cut frankfurters into 1-inch pieces. Thread frankfurters, onions and apples on cocktail skewers. Broil over low coals until frankfurters are heated through, brushing frequently with sauce.

Recipes for this photograph on page 89.

HIBACHI FRANKS

1 8-oz. can crushed pineapple
1 lg. onion, finely chopped
2 tbsp. oil
1/4 c. (firmly packed) brown sugar
1 tbsp. prepared mustard
1 tbsp. Worcestershire sauce
2 tbsp. vinegar
2 tbsp. dry mustard
Dash of salt
Dash of paprika
1/2 c. heavy cream, whipped
Canned cocktail frankfurters
Pineapple chunks

Drain pineapple, reserving 1/2 cup syrup. Cook onion in oil until soft. Add pineapple, reserved pineapple syrup, brown sugar, mustard, Worcestershire sauce and vinegar. Bring to a boil; reduce heat. Simmer for about 10 minutes. Keep warm over hibachi. Mix dry mustard and enough water to make thin paste; fold mustard, salt and paprika into whipped cream. Serve mustard sauce at room temperature. Spear cocktail franks and pineapple with toothpicks; grill over hibachi. Dip into mustard sauce.

BEACH KABOBS

4 smoked thuringer or knockwurst sausage
12 1 1/2-in. green pepper squares
12 tomato wedges
Melted butter

Cut each sausage crosswise into 3 pieces. Thread 3 pieces of sausage alternately with green pepper and tomato on each skewer. Grill 5 to 6 inches from coals for 10 to 12 minutes. Turn frequently, brushing with butter. Yield: 4 servings.

NIPPY BUTTER-CHEESE SPREAD

1 c. shredded Cheddar cheese,
   at room temperature
1/4 c. butter
1 tsp. prepared horseradish
1/2 tsp. prepared mustard
Rye bread

Recipes for this photograph on page 85.

Beat together cheese and butter until smooth in small mixing bowl. Beat in horseradish and mustard. Spread mixture on each slice of bread; close. Wrap each sandwich in foil. Heat on grill. Yield: 1 cup.

SAUCEPAN BROWNIES

1/2 c. butter
2 sq. unsweetened chocolate
1 c. sugar
2 eggs, beaten
1 tsp. vanilla
3/4 c. all-purpose flour
1/2 c. chopped walnuts
1/2 c. semisweet chocolate pieces

Melt butter and chocolate over low heat, stirring occasionally in 2-quart saucepan. Stir in sugar; cool to room temperature. Stir in eggs and vanilla. Add flour and walnuts. Turn into pan. Bake at 350 degrees for 25 to 30 minutes. Immediately sprinkle chocolate pieces over top; allow to stand 5 to 10 minutes or until melted. Spread as for frosting. Cool on wire rack; cut into squares.

Photograph for these recipes on page 87.

SAUCY BARBECUED CHICKEN

1 lg. onion, minced
1/2 clove of garlic, minced
1/4 c. catsup
2 tbsp. Worcestershire sauce
1 1/4 tsp. salt
Juice of 1 lemon
1/2 tbsp. sugar
1/2 tbsp. butter
Dash of pepper
1/3 c. vinegar
1 can tomato soup
1 c. water
1 frying chicken, disjointed

Combine all ingredients except chicken in saucepan. Bring to a boil. Reduce heat; simmer for 15 minutes. Place chicken pieces on grill 4 inches above coals. Cook for about 1 hour or until chicken is tender, turning and basting frequently.

PATIO SPECIAL

2 c. ground wieners
1/3 c. grated cheese
2 hard-cooked eggs, chopped
3 tbsp. chili sauce
2 tbsp. pickle relish
1 tsp. prepared mustard
1/2 tsp. garlic salt
Wiener buns

Combine wieners, cheese, eggs, chili sauce, pickle relish, mustard and salt. Split buns almost through. Spread wiener mixture on buns. Wrap buns separately in foil. Place on grill over low coals. Cook until heated through, turning frequently. Serve warm.

BUTTERFLIED LEG OF LAMB

1 4 to 5-lb. leg of lamb
1 c. soy sauce
1 tsp. ginger
2 tbsp. brown sugar
Pinch of basil
Barbecue sauce

Bone lamb; cut to lie flat. Combine soy sauce, ginger, brown sugar and basil. Marinate lamb for at least 2 hours or longer with soy sauce mixture. Place over hot coals. Broil for 1 hour to 1 hour and 30 minutes, turning occasionally. Baste with barbecue sauce. Cut across grain into thick slices.

CHILI-BARBECUED CHICKEN

3 2 to 2 1/2-lb. broiler chickens
1 c. hot water
5 tsp. salt
1/3 c. melted margarine
1 tsp. chili powder
1 tsp. seasoning salt

Wash chickens; split in half lengthwise. Mix hot water and salt. Place chickens over slow charcoal fire. Cook for 1 hour and 30 minutes to 2 hours, turning and basting with hot water frequently. Mix margarine with chili powder and seasoning salt. Brush over chicken several times 10 minutes before cooking time is up. Serve hot. Yield: 6 servings.

CHICKEN ON A GRILL

1 broiling chicken, disjointed
5 tbsp. A-1 sauce
1 8-oz. can tomato sauce
2 tbsp. brown sugar
2 tbsp. salad oil
1 c. melted butter

Place chicken in baking pan; cover. Bake at 350 degrees for 30 minutes. Mix A-1 sauce, tomato sauce, brown sugar and oil. Place hot chicken on charcoal grill. Cook until almost done, turning and basting with butter. Cook for 10 minutes longer, basting with tomato sauce mixture. Yield: 4 servings.

MARINADE FOR GRILLED CHICKEN

2 c. Worcestershire sauce
1 c. oil
1 c. white vinegar
1 c. wine vinegar
1 tsp. garlic powder
1/4 c. liquid smoke
1 tbsp. monosodium glutamate
3 pkg. dry Italian dressing mix
2 lemons, thinly sliced
1 tbsp. salt
1/2 tbsp. pepper

Combine all marinade ingredients in large shallow container; add chicken. Marinate at room temperature for 4 hours or in refrigerator for 8 to 12 hours. Use marinade as basting sauce when grilling chicken. Remove lemon from any remaining marinade. Refrigerate for future use.

GRILLED CORNISH HENS

1/4 c. salad oil
1/2 c. frozen orange juice
1/2 c. meat or giblet stock
2 tbsp. lemon juice
2 tsp. soy sauce
1 clove of garlic, crushed
1 tsp. salt
1/2 tsp. ginger
4 Rock Cornish hens

BARBECUED CATFISH

6 med. catfish
1 tsp. Worcestershire sauce
1/8 tsp. paprika
1/2 c. salad oil
1/4 c. white vinegar
1/4 c. catsup
2 tbsp. sugar
1/4 tsp. salt
1/4 tsp. pepper

Clean, skin and fillet catfish. Combine remaining ingredients for sauce; mix well. Brush catfish with sauce. Place on well-greased grill 3 to 4 inches above hot coals. Cook for 5 minutes on each side or until easily flaked, brushing frequently with sauce. Yield: 6 servings.

CHARCOAL-BROILED SALMON

1 6-lb. whole silver salmon, dressed
Slivered almonds to taste
Melted butter
Paprika to taste
Salt to taste
Pepper to taste

Cut salmon in half lengthwise. Combine almonds and 3 tablespoons butter; keep warm. Sprinkle paprika, salt and pepper on cut sides of salmon. Place salmon on charcoal grill, meat side down. Sear for 3 to 4 minutes. Place enough aluminum foil over top of salmon to cover skin; turn foil-covered side over. Brush butter over seared meat. Add almonds. Place aluminum foil quickly over salmon to hold in heat. Raise grill to 4 inches above coals. Cook for about 20 minutes or until salmon flakes easily.

Combine oil, orange juice, meat stock, lemon juice, soy sauce, garlic, salt and ginger. Pour mixture over hens. Marinate for at least 1 hour. Remove hens from marinade, reserving marinade. Tie wings and legs to bodies of hens; balance hens on spit. Cook for about 1 hour, brushing occasionally with reserved marinade.

PATIO-GRILLED TROUT

Trout
Bacon

Wrap trout with desired amount of bacon; fasten with wooden picks. Place on rack; cook, turning once, over coals until bacon is crisp. Damp hickory chips may be placed on coals if hickory flavor is desired. Serve with melted butter sauce.

BARBECUED BASS

1 4-lb. bass
2 tbsp. salad oil
2 tbsp. vinegar
1/2 c. catsup
1/4 c. water
1/2 c. onion, finely diced
1 clove of garlic, minced
2 tsp. Worcestershire sauce
2 drops of hot sauce
1 tsp. salt
1/4 tsp. pepper
1/4 tsp. dry mustard
1/2 tsp. chili powder
1 6-oz. can broiled in butter mushrooms

Place bass on double sheet of heavy-duty foil; bring foil up around fish. Combine remaining ingredients; heat. Pour hot sauce over fish. Fold foil securely. Place on grill 4 inches above coals. Cook for 25 to 30 minutes or until fish flakes easily.

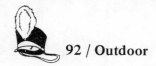

SAUCY GRILLED TROUT

1/4 c. French dressing
1 tbsp. lemon juice
1 tsp. salt
1/4 tsp. pepper
6 dressed trout

Combine French dressing, lemon juice, salt and pepper; mix well. Brush trout inside and out with sauce. Place trout on well-greased grill. Grill over moderately hot coals for 15 minutes. Turn; brush with sauce. Grill for 15 minutes longer or until fish flakes easily.

SOUTHERN-GRILLED TROUT

Salt and pepper to taste
4 lg. speckled trout
1/2 c. melted butter
1/3 c. lemon juice
5 tbsp. chopped parsley
1/2 c. grated onion
1/2 tsp. paprika
5 tbsp. Worcestershire sauce
1/8 tsp. cayenne pepper

Salt and pepper trout. Place each trout on foil square. Mix remaining ingredients; pour over trout. Close foil securely. Grill over hot coals, turning occasionally, for 30 minutes or until fish flakes easily.

LAWALU WHITEFISH

1 3 to 4-lb. whitefish
1/8 tsp. salt
2 slices bacon

Split whitefish in half. Sprinkle with salt. Place bacon between whitefish halves. Wrap whitefish in foil. Cook over hot coals for 30 minutes or until fish flakes easily with a fork.

PARTY LOBSTER-BEEF KABOBS

3 9-oz. packages frozen lobster tails
1 3/4-lb. 1-in. thick round steak
1/4 c. salad oil
1/4 c. wine vinegar
2 tbsp. lemon juice
1/4 c. tomato juice
1/2 tsp. garlic powder
1/8 tsp. pepper
1/2 tsp. salt
Dash of cayenne pepper
Unseasoned meat tenderizer

Thaw lobster tails. Trim away undersides of shells with scissors. Remove meat; cut into bite-sized pieces. Slice steak into 1/4-inch strips; cut crosswise into 1-inch pieces. Place lobster and steak in shallow dish. Combine all remaining ingredients except tenderizer in jar with tightfitting lid; shake well. Pour over lobster and steak. Marinate in refrigerator for 2 hours. Drain, reserving marinade; separate steak from lobster. Sprinkle steak with tenderizer. Thread lobster and steak alternately on 12 small skewers or hibachi sticks. Brush with reserved marinade. Place cake rack over grill. Arrange kabobs on rack. Grill 5 inches from source of heat for 6 to 7 minutes, turning occasionally and brushing with marinade. Yield: 12 servings.

BARBECUED LOBSTER

Cooked lobster, cut into 1 1/2-in. pieces
Barbecue sauce

Marinate lobster in barbecue sauce to cover for several hours. Thread pieces on skewers. Broil 3 inches from source of heat until browned lightly.

SAUCY LOBSTER GRILL

6 rock lobster tails
1 clove of garlic, mashed
Juice of 1 lemon
1 c. tomato juice
1/2 c. butter

Cut through middle of lobster shell with sharp knife. Cut through flesh but not underside membrane. Grasp tail in both hands; open flat, exposing meaty sections. Combine remaining ingredients in saucepan. Simmer until butter is melted. Place lobster, fleshy side down, on grill over 5 inches from source of heat. Cook for 5 minutes. Turn lobster; brush well with sauce. Cook until flesh is opaque, brushing several times with sauce. Brush with sauce just before serving.

STUFFED LOBSTER

    3 lobsters, each weighing 1 1/2 pounds
1 6-oz. package white and wild rice mix
1 c. sliced celery
2 tbsp. capers
4 slices American cheese, cut into
    1/2-in. cubes

Drop lobsters into boiling salted water. Cook only until water just reboils and lobster begins to turn bright red. Drain; drench with cold water. Cool. Cook rice mix according to package directions in a skillet placed on grill rack. Cook rice until tender and liquid absorbed. Stir in celery and capers. Slash underside of lobster lengthwise down the center with a sharp knife; open cut. Remove tail meat; dice. Stir lobster meat and cheese into rice mixture. Use mixture to stuff lobsters in slashed center. Turn the end of the tail up and over the stuffing; fasten in place with a metal skewer. Turn claws up; fasten in place with skewers. Place stuffed lobster on lower rack of steamer grill. Place a pan of water in bottom of grill; cover. Cook for 30 to 35 minutes or until piping hot. Yield: 6 servings.

Photograph for this recipe on page 80.

BARBECUED SHRIMP KABOBS

    12 slices bacon
1 lb. cooked shrimp
1 4-oz. can mushrooms, drained
1 can pineapple chunks, drained
1/4 c. soy sauce
1/4 c. salad oil
1/4 c. lemon juice
1/4 c. chopped parsley
1/2 tsp. salt
Dash of pepper

Fry bacon until cooked but not crisp; cut each slice in half. Alternate shrimp, mushrooms, pineapple and bacon on long skewers until skewers are filled. Combine all remaining ingredients. Brush kabobs generously with sauce. Place on grill 4 inches from source of heat. Broil for 3 minutes; turn, brush with sauce. Broil for 3 minutes longer or until browned lightly. Yield: 4 servings.

CHARCOALED MARINATED SHRIMP

    2 lb. shrimp in shells
3 cloves of chopped garlic
1 med. onion, chopped
1 tsp. dry mustard
1 tsp. salt
1/2 c. olive or peanut oil
3 tbsp. lemon juice
1/2 c. chopped parsley
1 tsp. dry basil (opt.)

Rinse shrimp; snip shell down back. Combine remaining ingredients. Pour over shrimp. Marinate shrimp for at least 5 hours. Place shrimp on grill over hot fire. Cook 5 to 8 minutes, turning once. Serve in shell with plenty of napkins. Yield: 4 servings.

SHRIMP KABOBS

    2 lb. jumbo shrimp, shelled and
    deveined
12 sm. plum tomatoes
2 green peppers, seeded and cut into
    1 1/2-in. pieces
12 mushrooms
3 zucchini, cut into 1/2-in. thick
    slices
1/2 c. oil
1/2 c. orange juice
1/4 c. lemon juice
1 sm. onion, grated
1 tsp. salt
1/4 tsp. pepper
2 tsp. paprika

Spear shrimp, tomatoes, peppers, mushrooms and zucchini on heatproof skewers. Place filled skewers into shallow glass or enamel pan. Mix remaining ingredients until thick. Pour mixture evenly over skewers. Marinate at least 2 hours. Drain skewers. Place on top layer of steamer grill; cover. Cook for 15 to 20 minutes or until vegetables are tender but still crisp. Yield: 6 servings.

Photograph for this recipe on page 80.

Substitutions and Cooking Guides

WHEN YOU'RE MISSING AN INGREDIENT . . .

Substitute 1 teaspoon dried herbs for 1 tablespoon fresh herbs.

Add 1/4 teaspoon baking soda and 1/2 cup buttermilk to equal 1 teaspoon baking powder. The buttermilk will replace 1/2 cup of the liquid indicated in the recipe.

Use 3 tablespoons dry cocoa plus 1 tablespoon butter or margarine instead of 1 square (1 ounce) unsweetened chocolate.

Make custard with 1 whole egg rather than 2 egg yolks.

Mix 1/2 cup evaporated milk with 1/2 cup water (or 1 cup reconstituted nonfat dry milk with 1 tablespoon butter) to replace 1 cup whole milk.

Make 1 cup of sour milk by letting stand for 5 minutes 1 tablespoon lemon juice or vinegar plus sweet milk to make 1 cup.

Substitute 1 package (2 teaspoons) active dry yeast for 1 cake compressed yeast.

Add 1 tablespoon instant minced onion, rehydrated, to replace 1 small fresh onion.

Substitute 1 tablespoon prepared mustard for 1 teaspoon dry mustard.

Use 1/8 teaspoon garlic powder instead of 1 small pressed clove of garlic.

Substitute 2 tablespoons of flour for 1 tablespoon of cornstarch to use as a thickening agent.

Mix 1/2 cup tomato sauce with 1/2 cup of water to make 1 cup tomato juice.

Make catsup or chili with 1 cup tomato sauce plus 1/2 cup sugar and 2 tablespoons vinegar.

CAN SIZE CHART

8 oz. can or jar	1 c.	1 lb. 4 oz. or 1 pt. 2 fl. oz. or No. 2 can or jar	2 1/2 c.
10 1/2 oz. can (picnic can)	1 1/4 c.	1 lb. 13 oz. can or jar or No. 2 1/2 can or jar	3 1/2 c.
12 oz. can (vacuum)	1 1/2 c.		
14-16 oz. or No. 300 can	1 1/4 c.	1 qt. 14 fl. oz. or 3 lb. 3 oz. or 46 oz. can	5 3/4 c.
16-17 oz. can or jar or No. 303 can or jar	2 c.	6 1/2 to 7 1/2 lb. or No. 10 can	12-13 c.

SUBSTITUTIONS

1 square *chocolate* (1 ounce) = 3 or 4 tablespoons cocoa plus 1/2 tablespoon fat.
1 tablespoon *cornstarch* (for thickening) = 2 tablespoons flour (approximately).
1 cup sifted *all-purpose flour* = 1 cup plus 2 tablespoons sifted cake flour.
1 cup sifted *cake flour* = 1 cup minus 2 tablespoons sifted all-purpose flour.
1 teaspoon *baking powder* = 1/4 teaspoon baking soda plus 1/2 teaspoon cream of tartar.
1 cup *bottled milk* = 1/2 cup evaporated milk plus 1/2 cup water.
1 cup *sour milk* = 1 cup sweet milk into which 1 tablespoon vinegar or lemon juice has been stirred; or 1 cup buttermilk.
1 cup *sweet milk* = 1 cup sour milk or buttermilk plus 1/2 teaspoon baking soda.
1 cup *canned tomatoes* = about 1 1/3 cups cut-up fresh tomatoes, simmered 10 minutes.
3/4 cup *cracker crumbs* = 1 cup bread crumbs.
1 cup *cream, sour, heavy* = 1/3 cup butter and 2/3 cup milk in any sour milk recipe.
1 cup *cream, sour, thin* = 3 tablespoons butter and 3/4 cup milk in sour milk recipe.
1 cup *molasses* = 1 cup honey.

Metric Conversion Chart

VOLUME

1 tsp.	=	4.9 cc
1 tbsp.	=	14.7 cc
1/3 c.	=	28.9 cc
1/8 c.	=	29.5 cc
1/4 c.	=	59.1 cc
1/2 c.	=	118.3 cc
3/4 c.	=	177.5 cc
1 c.	=	236.7 cc
2 c.	=	473.4 cc
1 fl. oz.	=	29.5 cc
4 oz.	=	118.3 cc
8 oz.	=	236.7 cc

1 pt.	=	473.4 cc
1 qt.	=	.946 liters
1 gal.	=	3.7 liters

CONVERSION FACTORS:

Liters	X	1.056	=	Liquid quarts
Quarts	X	0.946	=	Liters
Liters	X	0.264	=	Gallons
Gallons	X	3.785	=	Liters
Fluid ounces	X	29.563	=	Cubic centimeters
Cubic centimeters	X	0.034	=	Fluid ounces
Cups	X	236.575	=	Cubic centimeters
Tablespoons	X	14.797	=	Cubic centimeters
Teaspoons	X	4.932	=	Cubic centimeters
Bushels	X	0.352	=	Hectoliters
Hectoliters	X	2.837	=	Bushels

WEIGHT

1 dry oz.	=	28.3 Grams
1 lb.	=	.454 Kilograms

CONVERSION FACTORS:

Ounces (Avoir.)	X	28.349	=	Grams
Grams	X	0.035	=	Ounces
Pounds	X	0.454	=	Kilograms
Kilograms	X	2.205	=	Pounds

Equivalent Chart

3 tsp. = 1 tbsp.	16 oz. = 1 lb.	4 c. sifted flour = 1 lb.
2 tbsp. = 1/8 c.	1 oz. = 2 tbsp. fat or liquid	1 lb. butter = 2 c. or 4 sticks
4 tbsp. = 1/4 c.	2 c. fat = 1 lb.	2 pt. = 1 qt.
8 tbsp. = 1/2 c.	2 c. = 1 pt.	1 qt. = 4 c.
16 tbsp. = 1 c.	2 c. sugar = 1 lb.	A Few Grains = Less than 1/8 tsp.
5 tbsp. + 1 tsp. = 1/3 c.	5/8 c. = 1/2 c. + 2 tbsp.	Pinch is as much as can be taken
12 tbsp. = 3/4 c.	7/8 c. = 3/4 c. + 2 tbsp.	between tip of finger and thumb.
4 oz. = 1/2 c.	2 2/3 c. powdered sugar = 1 lb.	Speck = Less than 1/8 tsp.
8 oz. = 1 c.	2 2/3 c. brown sugar = 1 lb.	

WHEN YOU NEED APPROXIMATE MEASUREMENTS . . .

1 lemon makes 3 tablespoons juice
1 lemon makes 1 teaspoon grated peel
1 orange makes 1/3 cup juice
1 orange makes about 2 teaspoons grated peel
1 chopped medium onion makes 1/2 cup pieces
1 pound unshelled walnuts makes 1 1/2 to 1 3/4 cups shelled
1 pound unshelled almonds makes 3/4 to 1 cup shelled
8 to 10 egg whites make 1 cup

12 to 14 egg yolks make 1 cup
1 pound shredded American cheese makes 4 cups
1/4 pound crumbled blue cheese makes 1 cup
1 cup unwhipped cream makes 2 cups whipped
4 ounces (1 to 1 1/4 cups) uncooked macaroni makes 2 1/4 cups cooked
7 ounces spaghetti make 4 cups cooked
4 ounces (1 1/2 to 2 cups) uncooked noodles make 2 cups cooked.

MAKE 1 CUP OF FINE CRUMBS WITH . . .

28 saltine crackers
4 slices bread
14 square graham crackers
22 vanilla wafers

NUTRITION LABELING CHART

High School teenagers today are probably more aware of good nutrition than their age has ever been before. They learn about it in the classroom, read about it in the newspapers, and hear about it on television all the time. For that reason, the High School Choral Groups and Band Members who are presenting this book to you believe it would not be complete without a *Nutrition Labeling Chart,* as well as an explanation of what it's all about. Homemakers who are concerned about good nutrition want to know how much food value they are getting for their dollar. Moreover, the cook who has to prepare a strict diet for a diabetic must know the carbohydrate gram content of a food, while another cook may have to know how many milligrams of sodium a certain food product contains. Whether a person merely wants to know, or whether a person *needs* to know for the sake of his health, nutrition labeling is probably one of the greatest services commercial food manufacturers have done for the consumer in years.

NUTRITION CHART

The United States Food and Drug Administration has determined how much of every key nutrient is needed by the average healthy adult, well known as the Recommended Daily Dietary Allowance (RDA). The United States RDA reflects the highest amounts of nutrients for all ages and sexes. Pregnant women, nursing mothers, as well as persons with special dietary needs should consult their doctor for any recommended increases or decreases in their daily diet.

UNITED STATES RECOMMENDED DAILY ALLOWANCE CHART

Protein . . . . .45-65 Grams
Carbohydrates . . . . .125 Grams
Vitamin A . . . . .5,000 International Units
Thiamine (Vitamin B_1) . . . . .1.5 Milligrams
Riboflavin (Vitamin B_2) . . . . .1.7 Milligrams
Vitamin B_6 . . . . 2 Milligrams
Vitamin B_{12} . . . . .6 Micrograms
Folic Acid (B Vitamin) . . . . 0.4 Milligrams
Pantothenic Acid (B Vitamin) . . . . .10 Milligrams
Vitamin C (Ascorbic Acid) . . . . 55-60 Milligrams
Vitamin D . . . . 400 International Units

Vitamin E . . . . 30 International Units
Iron . . . . 18 Milligrams
Calcium . . . . .1 Gram
Niacin (Nicotinic Acid) . . . . .13-20 Milligrams
Magnesium .400 Milligrams
Zinc . . . . 15 Milligrams
Copper . . . . 2 Milligrams
Phosphorus . . . . .1 Gram
Iodine . . . . 150 Micrograms
Biotin (Vitamin H) . . . . 0.3 Milligrams

---

IMPORTANT NUTRIENTS YOUR DIET REQUIRES

PROTEIN

Why? Absolutely essential in building, repairing and renewing of all body tissue. Helps body resist infection. Builds enzymes and hormones, helps form and maintain body fluids.

Where? Milk, eggs, lean meats, poultry, fish, soybeans, peanuts, dried peas and beans, grains and cereals.

CARBOHYDRATES

Why?   Provide needed energy for bodily functions, provide warmth, as well as fuel for brain and nerve tissues. Lack of carbohydrates will cause body to use protein for energy rather than for repair and building.

Where?   Sugars: sugar, table syrups, jellies and jams, etc., as well as dried and fresh fruits. Starches: cereals, pasta, rice, corn, dried beans and peas, potatoes, stem and leafy vegetables, and milk.

FATS

Why?   Essential in the use of fat soluble vitamins (A, D, E, K), and fatty acids. Have more than twice the concentrated energy than equal amounts of carbohydrate for body energy and warmth.

Where?   Margarine, butter, cooking oil, mayonnaise, vegetable shortening, milk, cream, ice cream, cheese, meat, fish, eggs, poultry, chocolate, coconut, nuts.

VITAMIN A

Why?   Needed for healthy skin and hair, as well as for healthy, infection-resistant mucous membranes.

Where?   Dark green, leafy and yellow vegetables, liver. Deep yellow fruits, such as apricots and cantaloupe. Milk, cheese, eggs, as well as fortified margarine and butter.

THIAMINE (VITAMIN B_1)

Why?   Aids in the release of energy of foods, as well as in normal appetite and digestion. Promotes healthy nervous system.

Where?   Pork, liver, kidney. Dried peas and beans. Whole grain and enriched breads and cereals.

RIBOFLAVIN (VITAMIN B_2)

Why?   Helps to oxidize foods. Promotes healthy eyes and skin, especially around mouth and eyes. Prevents pellagra.

Where?   Meats, especially liver and kidney, as well as milk, cheese, eggs. Dark green leafy vegetables. Enriched bread and cereal products. Almonds, dried peas and beans.

VITAMIN B_6

Why?   Helps protein in building body tissues. Needed for healthy nerves, skin and digestion. Also helps body to use fats and carbohydrates for energy.

Where?   Milk, wheat germ, whole grain and fortified cereals. Liver, kidney, pork and beef.

VITAMIN B_{12}

Why?   Aids body in formation of red blood cells, as well as in regular work of all body cells.

Where?   Lean meats, milk, eggs, fish, cheese, as well as liver and kidney.

FOLIC ACID

Why?   Aids in healthy blood system, as well as intestinal tract. Helps to prevent anemia.

Where?   Green leaves of vegetables and herbs, as well as liver and milk. Wheat germ and soybeans.

PANTOTHENIC ACID

Why?   Aids in proper function of digestive system.

Where?   Liver, kidney and eggs. Peanuts and molasses. Broccoli and other vegetables.

VITAMIN C (ASCORBIC ACID)

Why?   Promotes proper bone and tooth formation. Helps body utilize iron and resist infection. Strengthens blood vessels. Lack of it causes bones to heal slowly, failure of wounds to heal and fragile vessels to bleed easily.

Where? Citrus fruits, cantaloupe and strawberries. Broccoli, kale, green peppers, raw cabbage, sweet potatoes, cauliflower, tomatoes.

VITAMIN D

Why? Builds strong bones and teeth by aiding utilization of calcium and phosphorus.
Where? Fortified milk, fish liver oils, as well as salmon, tuna and sardines. Also eggs.

VITAMIN E

Why? Needed in maintaining red blood cells.
Where? Whole grain cereals, wheat germ, beans and peas, lettuce and eggs.

IRON

Why? Used with protein for hemoglobin production. Forms nucleus of each cell, and helps them to use oxygen.
Where? Kidney and liver, as well as shellfish, lean meats, and eggs. Deep yellow and dark green leafy vegetables. Dried peas, beans and fruits. Potatoes, whole grain cereals and bread. Enriched flour and bread. Dark molasses.

CALCIUM

Why? Builds and renews bones, teeth and other tissues, as well as aids in the proper function of muscles, nerves and heart. Controls normal blood clotting. With protein, aids in oxidation of foods.
Where? Milk and milk products, excluding butter. Dark green vegetables, oysters, clams and sardines.

NIACIN

Why? Helps body to oxidize food. Aids in digestion, and helps to keep nervous system and skin healthy.
Where? Peanuts, liver, tuna, as well as fish, poultry and lean meats. Enriched breads, cereals and peas.

MAGNESIUM

Why? Aids nervous system and sleep.
Where? Almonds, peanuts, raisins and prunes. Vegetables, fruits, milk, fish and meats.

ZINC

Why? Needed for cell formation.
Where? Nuts and leafy green vegetables. Shellfish.

COPPER

Why? Helps body to utilize iron.
Where? Vegetables and meats.

PHOSPHORUS

Why? Maintains normal blood clotting function, as well as builds bones, teeth and nerve tissue. Aids in utilization of sugar and fats.
Where? Oatmeal and whole wheat products. Eggs and cheese, dried beans and peas. Nuts, lean meats, fish and poultry.

IODINE

Why? Enables thyroid gland to maintain proper body metabolism.
Where? Iodized salt. Saltwater fish and seafood. Milk and vegetables.

BIOTIN (VITAMIN H)

Why? Helps to maintain body cells.
Where? Eggs and liver. Any foods rich in Vitamin B.

Index

PHOTOGRAPH RECIPES

Order Form 70890

PLEASE SEND ME THE FOLLOWING BOOKS:
(NOTE: Music Groups & Schools should
request special discount order forms.)

Name

Address

City _____ State _____ Zip

☐ Enclosed is payment for full amount. No charge for postage and handling.

**MAIL TO: FAVORITE RECIPES PRESS/NASHVILLE EMS ORDER
PROCESSING • P.O. BOX 77 • NASHVILLE, TENNESSEE 37202**

Quan.	Cookbook Title	Item No.
	MEDLEY OF MEATS	01384A
	KITCHEN AUDITIONS	70408A

Order Form 70890

PLEASE SEND ME THE FOLLOWING BOOKS:
(NOTE: Music Groups & Schools should
request special discount order forms.)

Name

Address

City _____ State _____ Zip

☐ Enclosed is payment for full amount. No charge for postage and handling.

**MAIL TO: FAVORITE RECIPES PRESS/NASHVILLE EMS ORDER
PROCESSING • P.O. BOX 77 • NASHVILLE, TENNESSEE 37202**

Quan.	Cookbook Title	Item No.
	MEDLEY OF MEATS	01384A
	KITCHEN AUDITIONS	70408A

Order Form 70890

PLEASE SEND ME THE FOLLOWING BOOKS:
(NOTE: Music Groups & Schools should
request special discount order forms.)

Name

Address

City _____ State _____ Zip

☐ Enclosed is payment for full amount. No charge for postage and handling.

**MAIL TO: FAVORITE RECIPES PRESS/NASHVILLE EMS ORDER
PROCESSING • P.O. BOX 77 • NASHVILLE, TENNESSEE 37202**

Quan.	Cookbook Title	Item No.
	MEDLEY OF MEATS	01384A
	KITCHEN AUDITIONS	70408A